SPECTRUM

CALIFORNIA
Test Practice

D0761537

Frank Schaffer Publications®

SPECTRUM

Frank Schaffer Publications®

Spectrum is an imprint of Frank Schaffer Publications.

Send all inquiries to:
Frank Schaffer Publications
8720 Orion Place
Columbus, Ohio 43240-2111

ISBN 0-7696-3006-5

4 5 6 7 8 9 10 MAZ 12 11 10 09 08 07

Table of Contents

What's Inside?

This workbook is designed to help you and your sixth-grader understand what he or she will be expected to know on the California sixth-grade state tests.

Practice Pages

The workbook is divided into a Language Arts section and Mathematics section. Each section has practice activities that have questions similar to those that will appear on the state tests. Students should use a pencil to fill in the correct answers and to complete any writing on these activities.

California Content Standards

Before each practice section is a list of the state standards covered by that section. The shaded "What it means" sections will help to explain any information in the standards that might be unfamiliar.

Mini-Tests and Final Tests

Practice activities are grouped by state standard. When each group is completed, the student can move on to a *Mini-Test* that covers the material presented on those practice activities. After an entire set of standards and accompanying activities are completed, the student should take the *Final Tests,* which incorporate materials from all the practice activities in that section.

Final Test Answer Sheet

The Final Tests have a separate answer sheet that mimics the style of the answer sheet the students will use on the state tests. An answer sheet appears at the end of each Final Test.

How Am I Doing?

The *How Am I Doing?* pages are designed to help students identify areas where they are proficient and areas where they still need more practice. Students can keep track of each of their Mini-Test scores on these pages.

Answer Key

Answers to all the practice activities, mini-tests, and final tests are listed by page number and appear at the end of the book.

Frequently Asked Questions

What is STAR?

STAR stands for **S**tandardized **T**esting **A**nd **R**eporting program. It is the name used for the series of tests given to students in California schools.

What kinds of information does my student have to know to pass the test?

The California Department of Education has created a set of guidelines that list specific skills and information that students must know before moving on to the next grade. Each of these (called content standards, or learning outcomes) is listed in this workbook and clearly explained. Practice activities have been designed to test your sixth-grader's mastery of each California content standard.

Are there special strategies or tips that will help my student do well?

The workbook provides sample questions that have content similar to that on the **STAR** tests. Test-taking tips are offered throughout the book.

How do I know what areas my student needs help in?

A special **How Am I Doing?** section will help you and your sixth-grader evaluate progress. It will pinpoint areas where more work is needed as well as areas where your student excels.

California English-Language Content Standards

The English-language arts content standards developed by the California State Board of Education are divided into four major sections. The information within those sections tells specifically what your sixth-grader should know or be able to do.

1) Reading

1.0:   Word Analysis, Fluency, and Systematic Vocabulary Development

2.0:   Reading Comprehension

3.0:   Literary Response and Analysis

2) Writing

1.0:   Writing Strategies

2.0:   Writing Applications (Genres and Their Characteristics)

3) Written and Oral English Language Conventions

1.0:   Written and Oral English Language Conventions

4) Listening and Speaking

1.0:   Listening and Speaking Strategies

2.0:   Speaking Applications (Genres and Their Characteristics)

California Language Arts Table of Contents

Reading Standards

1.0 Word Analysis, Fluency, and Systematic Vocabulary Development

Students use their knowledge of word origins and word relationships, as well as historical and literary context clues, to determine the meaning of specialized vocabulary and to understand the precise meaning of grade-level-appropriate words.

Word Recognition

1.1 Read aloud narrative and expository text fluently and accurately and with appropriate pacing, intonation, and expression.

Vocabulary and Concept Development

1.2 Identify and interpret figurative language and words with multiple meanings. *(See page 8.)*

What it means:
- Figurative language is language used for descriptive effect. It describes or implies meaning, rather than directly stating it. Examples of figurative language include:

  similes - using *like* or *as* to compare things that may seem unlike each other. Example: Her smile was as dazzling as the sun.

  metaphors - comparing unlike things but without using *like* or *as*. Example: His body was a well-oiled machine.

  hyperbole - using exaggeration to convey strong emotion, express humor, or emphasize a point. Example: I felt like we walked a million miles!

  personification - assigning human qualities, feelings, or actions to an animal, an object, or an idea. Example: The mother bear cried for her cub.

1.3 Recognize the origins and meanings of frequently used foreign words in English and use these words accurately in speaking and writing. *(See page 9.)*

1.4 Monitor expository text for unknown words or words with novel meanings by using word, sentence, and paragraph clues to determine meaning. *(See page 10.)*

1.5 Understand and explain "shades of meaning" in related words (e.g., softly and quietly). *(See page 11.)*

Reading
1.2

Word Analysis, Fluency, and
Systematic Vocabulary
Development

Figurative Language and Words with Multiple Meanings

DIRECTIONS: Choose the best answer.

1. **Will you brush my hair? In which sentence does the word *brush* mean the same thing as in the sentence above?**

   (A) She bought a new brush.

   (B) After the storm, the yard was littered with brush.

   (C) I need to brush the dog.

   (D) She felt the kitten brush against her leg.

2. **He plans to store the corn in his barn. In which sentence does the word *store* mean the same thing as in the sentence above?**

   (F) She went to the grocery store.

   (G) My dad will store the lawn mower in the shed.

   (H) The owner will store his shelves with merchandise.

   (J) My favorite store is in the mall.

3. **Because of her fever, she felt faint. In which sentence does the word *faint* mean the same thing as in the sentence above?**

   (A) Her dress was a faint pink.

   (B) When he saw the blood, he felt faint.

   (C) The writing on the yellowing paper was very faint.

   (D) Her voice was so faint I could barely hear it.

DIRECTIONS: Chose the word that correctly completes both sentences.

4. **The second _____ of our encyclopedia set is missing.**
   Please turn down the _____ on your stereo.

   (F) sound

   (G) volume

   (H) book

   (J) dial

5. **The _____ piece goes here.**
   The first _____ of the tournament is over.

   (A) square

   (B) part

   (C) round

   (D) circular

6. **Did someone _____ the cookies?**
   Leather is the _____ of an animal.

   (F) eat

   (G) hide

   (H) skin

   (J) bake

STOP

Reading

Word Analysis, Fluency, and Systematic Vocabulary Development

1.3

Word Origins

Clue   Many of the words we use in English are actually borrowed from other languages.

DIRECTIONS: Answer the following questions about foreign words used in English.

1. **Which of these words probably comes from a French word meaning *fair-haired*?**
   - (A) brunette
   - (B) blond
   - (C) petite
   - (D) critique

2. **Which of these words probably comes from a Spanish word meaning *the lizard*?**
   - (F) horse
   - (G) cat
   - (H) dog
   - (W) alligator

3. **The German word *hamburger* means**
   _____ .
   - (A) ground beef patty
   - (B) sausage
   - (C) breaded
   - (D) restaurant

4. **Which of these words probably comes from a French word meaning *short*?**
   - (F) critique
   - (G) genre
   - (H) petite
   - (J) encore

5. **Which of these words probably comes from a German word meaning *preschool*?**
   - (A) encore
   - (B) patio
   - (C) kindergarten
   - (D) genre

6. **The French word *encore* means _____ .**
   - (F) again
   - (G) short
   - (H) type
   - (J) judgment

7. **Which of these words probably comes from the Middle English word *muflein* meaning *wrapped up*?**
   - (A) muffled
   - (B) mottled
   - (C) mounted
   - (D) molted

8. **Which of these words probably comes from the Middle English word *couchen* meaning *to lie down*?**
   - (F) cloud
   - (G) crowd
   - (H) catch
   - (J) crouch

STOP

Reading

| 1.4 |

Word Analysis, Fluency, and Systematic Vocabulary Development

Using Context Clues to Determine Meaning

Clue   If you aren't sure which answer is correct, substitute each answer in the blank.

DIRECTIONS: Read the paragraph. Find the word that fits best in each numbered blank. Fill in the circle for the correct answer.

> People who travel or cross the Amazon and Orinoco rivers of South America are careful never to _____ **(1)** a foot or hand from the side of their boat. For just below the surface of these mighty waters _____ **(2)** a small fish feared throughout the _____ **(3)**. That fish is the flesh-eating piranha. It has a nasty _____ **(4)** and an even nastier _____ **(5)**. Although smaller fish make up most of its diet, the piranha will _____ **(6)** both humans and other animals.

1. (A) lift
    (B) dangle
    (C) withdraw
    (D) brush

2. (F) lurks
    (G) nests
    (H) plays
    (J) boasts

3. (A) universe
    (B) town
    (C) continent
    (D) village

4. (F) habit
    (G) friend
    (H) flavor
    (J) disposition

5. (A) smile
    (B) brother
    (C) appetite
    (D) memory

6. (F) befriend
    (G) bully
    (H) attack
    (J) analyze

STOP

Name _____   Date _____

Reading

1.5

Understanding Shades of Meaning

DIRECTIONS: Read each item. Choose the answer that means the same or about the same as the underlined word. Fill in the circle for the correct answer.

1. **Prolong the agony**
   - (A) extend
   - (B) shorten
   - (C) stop
   - (D) postpone

2. **Scour the tub**
   - (F) preserve
   - (G) fill
   - (H) scrub
   - (J) lug

3. **Unruly behavior**
   - (A) ridiculous
   - (B) obedient
   - (C) calm
   - (D) willful

4. **Concealed the evidence**
   - (F) avoided
   - (G) revealed
   - (H) hid
   - (J) examined

5. **Her bias was plain to see.**
   - (A) point of view
   - (B) loss
   - (C) wisdom
   - (D) slip

6. **The boy had a hunch.**
   - (F) feeling
   - (G) bad attitude
   - (H) limp
   - (J) cramp

7. **The professor rambled.**
   - (A) got lost
   - (B) babbled
   - (C) argued
   - (D) stopped

8. **The twins mustered their courage.**
   - (F) lost
   - (G) faked
   - (H) proclaimed
   - (J) gathered

9. **A diminutive woman**
   - (A) tiny
   - (B) industrious
   - (C) slow
   - (D) energetic

10. **It was an ambush.**
    - (F) a courageous fight
    - (G) a surprise attack
    - (H) a change in plans
    - (J) a flowering plant

STOP

Reading

1.0

For pages 8–11

Word Analysis, Fluency, and Systematic Vocabulary Development

Mini-Test 1

Clue — An analogy is a set of word pairs that have a particular kind of relationship.

Word Bank

cloudless	melody	light	ordinary
red	stop	land	lass
permit	untidy	white	low
positive	foolish	lengthy	century

DIRECTIONS: To solve the analogies below, determine how the first pair of words is related. Then choose a word from the word bank that correctly completes the analogy.

1. **Quiet** is to **calm** as **silly** is to

_____

2. **Ten** is to **decade** as **hundred** is to

_____

3. **Foggy** is to **murky** as **clear** is to

_____

4. **Strange** is to **odd** as **usual** is to

_____

5. **Lavender** is to **purple** as **pink** is to

_____

6. **Liquid** is to **water** as **solid** is to

_____

7. **Cut** is to **sever** as **let** is to

_____

8. **Plain** is to **simple** as **song** is to

_____

9. **Out** is to **in** as **go** is to

_____

10. **Strong** is to **weak** as **heavy** is to

_____

11. **After** is to **before** as **high** is to

_____

12. **No** is to **yes** as **negative** is to

_____

13. **Boy** is to **girl** as **lad** is to

_____

14. **Smooth** is to **mussed** as **neat** is to

_____

Reading Standards

2.0 Reading Comprehension (Focus on Informational Materials)

Students read and understand grade-level-appropriate material. They describe and connect the essential ideas, arguments, and perspectives of the text by using their knowledge of text structure, organization, and purpose.

Structural Features of Informational Materials

2.1 Identify the structural features of popular media (e.g., newspapers, magazines, online information) and use the features to obtain information. *(See pages 14–15.)*

2.2 Analyze text that uses the compare-and-contrast organizational pattern. *(See pages 16–17.)*

Comprehension and Analysis of Grade-Level-Appropriate Text

2.3 Connect and clarify main ideas by identifying their relationships to other sources and related topics. *(See pages 18–19.)*

2.4 Clarify an understanding of texts by creating outlines, logical notes, summaries, or reports. *(See pages 20–21.)*

2.5 Follow multiple-step instructions for preparing applications (e.g., for a public library card, bank savings account, sports club, league membership). *(See page 22.)*

Expository Critique

What it means:
- Expository text conveys information or offers an explanation.

2.6 Determine the adequacy and appropriateness of the evidence for an author's conclusions. *(See pages 23–24.)*

2.7 Make reasonable assertions about a text through accurate, supporting citations. *(See pages 25–26.)*

2.8 Note instances of unsupported inferences, fallacious reasoning, persuasion, and propaganda in text. *(See pages 27–28.)*

Obtaining Information from the Popular Media

DIRECTIONS: Look at the newspaper page below and answer the following questions.

Monday, June 3

DAILY SENTINEL

Today's Weather— Sunny, high 82

INDEX

Firefighter Rescues Boy

This morning at 4:00 A.M., a fire erupted in a private residence located at 3345 Palmer Street. The family dog woke the family from their slumber with its insistent barking. All but the youngest son were able to escape from the home. Firefighters were on the scene within minutes after a neighbor alerted them. (Photo on page A5) In a daring move, a firefighter was able to rescue the young boy by (Continued on page A5)

Local Business Volunteers Aid

After the recent earthquake that left thousands homeless, a local business temporarily shut its doors and bused its employees to the scene of the devastation. The employees set up tents to serve hot meals and dispense food and clothing. Ron Wardie, owner of Supply Co., told reporters, "It was my employees' idea. I was reluctant at first. But they were so willing to donate their time, I couldn't help but say yes." (Continued on page A6)

1. **How many sections does this paper have?**

   (A) 1

   (B) 2

   (C) 3

   (D) 4

2. **Which of these appears on A5?**

   (F) weather

   (G) the continuation of the story about the firefighter

   (H) world news

   (J) the continuation of the story about the local business

3. **What was the weather on the day this newspaper was published?**

   (A) Cloudy with a high of 72

   (B) The weather is listed on D1.

   (C) Sunny with a high of 82

   (D) It can't be determined.

4. **In which section would you be most likely to find job listings?**

   (F) A

   (G) B

   (H) C

   (J) D

GO

5. **Where is the rest of the article about the volunteers?**

- (A) on the bottom of the page
- (B) page A2
- (C) page A6
- (D) page B6

6. **At what time did the fire break out?**

- (F) 4:00 A.M.
- (G) June 2
- (H) within minutes
- (J) 7:00 P.M.

7. **In what section would you find an article about the Palmer High Partners' last game?**

- (A) B1
- (B) A19
- (C) C6
- (D) D1

8. **In what section would you find an article about the new show on channel 4?**

- (F) A2
- (G) A21
- (H) A20
- (J) A19

9. **The employees of Supply Co. volunteered their time after what event?**

- (A) a fire
- (B) a flood
- (C) an earthquake
- (D) a tornado

10. **How was the family warned about the fire?**

- (F) a neighbor
- (G) a barking dog
- (H) an alarm
- (J) firefighters arrived

11. **Your sister wants to work the puzzles. In which section will she find them?**

- (A) A
- (B) B
- (C) C
- (D) D

12. **You mother wants to find out information about the merger of two local companies. In which section should she look?**

- (F) D
- (G) C
- (H) B
- (J) A

STOP

Comparing and Contrasting

Antarctica

Antarctica is the continent surrounding the South Pole. It contains 90 percent of the world's ice. Antarctica is the coldest and most desolate region on Earth. It covers 5,400,000 square miles. Much of the land is buried under snow and ice one mile thick. The winter temperatures reach -100°F in the interior of the continent. On the coast, the temperatures fall below -40°F.

The interior of Antarctica is a frozen, lifeless region. The only animal life in Antarctica is found on the coastline or in the sea. Penguins, seals, whales, and other fish and birds live in or close to the coastal waters. These animals live on food from the sea.

The ancient Greeks called the North Pole the "Arctic." They believed that land at the South Pole must also exist. They called this supposed land "Antarctica," meaning the opposite of Arctic.

In 1928, Commander Richard E. Byrd of the U.S. Navy led a famous expedition to the South Pole. He and his men set up a base called Little America. Until his death in 1957, Byrd took five expeditions to Antarctica. He helped establish scientific research bases and led the largest Antarctic expedition in history with over 4,000 men and 13 ships.

The Sahara

Stretching almost 3,000 miles across North Africa, the Sahara Desert is an incredible natural wonder of sand, rock, and gravel. The Sahara covers over 3,500,000 square miles, which makes it by far the largest desert on Earth. It extends west to east from the Atlantic Ocean to the Red Sea.

The name Sahara comes from an Arabic word, *Sahra*, which means desert. Because of the unusually low rainfall, the sun-scorched land and blistering winds make the Sahara the hottest region in the world during the summer. A sandy surface may reach a temperature of 170°F. The cloudless skies allow the daytime air temperature to reach 100°F. At night, the temperature often drops 40 to 50 degrees.

The Sahara's only vegetation is found near wells, springs, or streams. These fertile areas are called oases. Throughout the desert are many dry streambeds, called *wadis*. During a rare rain, they temporarily fill up with water. The Sahara supports some animal life, too—camels, lizards, and the addax, a desert antelope.

Some people of the Sahara live in tents, which allows them to move more easily in search of grassy areas. These people, called nomads, tend flocks of sheep, camels, or goats. Other people raise crops on land that has been irrigated.

GO →

Name _____   Date _____

DIRECTIONS: Answer the following questions comparing Antarctica and the Sahara.

1. **What challenges are presented by both regions because of their climate?**

   Both regions are either very cold or very hot. They both have scarce food.

2. **How have humans and/or animals adapted to life in both regions?**

   Humans and animals who live in Antartica are very cold but they have either a lot of fur, Rubber, or coats. Now human and animals in the Sahara are very hot they either have coldblood lot's of water or now how to produce their own shade.

3. **If you had to choose to go on an expedition to either Antarctica or the Sahara, which place would you choose? Why?**

   I would go to Antartica. Because there is water unlike the Sahara. And fish. Sure it may be cold but you can just wear more clothes.

Identifying Main Ideas

The Stanley Cup

Today, one of the most popular spectator sports in the world is ice hockey. Each year, the teams of the National Hockey League play a series of games to determine who will win the championship of ice hockey. The winner is presented an award called the Stanley Cup. The Stanley Cup is one of the most prestigious awards in the world of sports.

Ice hockey is now an international sport. But nowhere is hockey more popular than in Canada. Over 125 years ago, hockey-on-ice was played in Montreal, Canada. In 1870, the first official rules of the game were written. By 1880, official teams were organized into leagues.

Some of the first league games were played on town ice rinks that had bandstands right in the middle of the rinks! Later, special ice hockey rinks were built that even featured lights hung from telegraph poles.

The popularity of the game seemed to sweep through Canada. One of hockey's greatest fans was Lord Stanley of Preston, the sixth Governor General of Canada. Lord Stanley organized a championship game in which Canadian ice hockey teams would compete.

On March 22, 1894, the first Stanley Cup game was played in Montreal, Canada, at Victoria Rink. The championship game received its name from the award presented to the winner. Donated by Lord Stanley, the first award was a sterling silver cup.

The original Stanley Cup has gone through several changes over the years. Bands were added on the bottom of the bowl to hold the names of more winners. After many years of wear, the original cup was retired to the Hockey Hall of Fame in 1969.

After that first championship game in 1894, the game of ice hockey continued to grow in popularity. Today, the National Hockey League includes teams from America as well as Canada. The Montreal Canadiens hold the record for winning the most Stanley Cup championships. Each year, a new set of teams plays a series of games to determine who wins the championship of ice hockey and the Stanley Cup.

GO

Name _____   Date _____

DIRECTIONS: Choose the best answer.

1. **Which sentence best summarizes the main idea of this passage?**

   (A) Americans do not like hockey as much as Canadians.

   (B) The Stanley Cup was given to the winner of the first championship game.

   (C) The rules of ice hockey were written in Canada.

   (D) The Stanley Cup is a symbol of Canada's love of ice hockey.

2. **Which statement about the Stanley Cup is not true?**

   (F) It was named after Lord Stanley.

   (G) It is given to the ice hockey championship winner.

   (H) The original cup has never changed.

   (J) The Montreal Canadiens hold the record for winning it the most.

3. **In what year were ice hockey teams organized into leagues?**

   (A) 1870

   (B) 1880

   (C) 1894

   (D) 1900

DIRECTIONS: Write a *T* if the statement is true and an *F* if the statement is false. Ice hockey—

4. ___F___ **is only played in the Stanley Sports Center.**

5. ___T___ **teams of the National League play a series of games for the championship.**

6. ___T___ **is now an international sport.**

7. ___F___ **was probably first played in France.**

8. ___T___ **is probably most popular in Canada.**

DIRECTIONS: Fill in the answers to the following questions.

9. **When was the first Stanley Cup game played?**

   _____1894_____

10. **In what city was the first Stanley Cup game played?**

    _____Montreal_____

11. **Lord Stanley held what position in Canadian government?**

    ___sixth governer goverment___

12. **The original Stanley Cup was retired in what year?**

    _____1969_____

© Frank Schaffer Publications

Summarizing

Decathlon

The decathlon is one of the most famous contests in sports. *Decathlon* is a Greek word that means "ten contests." The first decathlon was added to the Olympic Games in 1912. It was added in honor of athletes who competed in the original Olympic Games in Greece. Most of the games in the early Olympics were contests of running, jumping, and throwing. Today, these kinds of events are called track and field events.

A decathlon is a two-day contest that features ten separate events in track and field. The events for the first day are the 100-meter dash, long jump, shot put, high jump, and 400-meter run. The events for the second day are the 110-meter hurdles, discus throw, pole vault, javelin throw, and 1500-meter run.

The 100-meter dash starts the decathlon. It takes just seconds for the athletes to run the 100-meter race, which is approximately the length of a football field.

An athlete has three chances for a high score in the long jump and high jump. The best score out of three attempts is used.

The shot put is an event that requires a tremendous amount of power to throw a 16-pound metal ball, called a shot, as far as possible.

The final event of the first day is the 400-meter run. This race is almost a quarter of a mile in length. It is a hard race to run because it is too long to run in one burst of energy. But it is too short to run at a slower pace. Some people have called this the "murderous race."

The second day begins with the 110-meter hurdles. The runners must not only run fast, but also jump over ten hurdles, which are three-and-a-half feet tall.

The discus throw is an event in which an athlete throws a four-pound metal plate, called a discus, as far as possible.

The pole vault is one of the hardest events of the decathlon. An athlete runs and lifts himself or herself high into the air on a pole. The aim is to jump over a high bar without knocking it down.

The javelin throw event requires an athlete to throw a javelin, a kind of spear, as far as possible.

The final event is the 1,500-meter run. It is a little less than a mile long. The goal of every decathlon athlete is to win the gold medal in the Olympic Games. The winner is often called "the world's greatest athlete."

GO

DIRECTIONS: Complete the charts below to summarize the events of the decathlon.

Decathlon Events by Day

First Day	Second Day
1. 100 m dash	6. 110 m hurdles
2. long jump	7. discus throw
3. shot put	8. pole vault
4. high jump	9. javelin throw
5. 400 m run	10. 1500 m run

	Name of Events	Description
11.	discus throw	An athlete throws a four-pound metal plate as far as possible.
12.	100 meter dash	This race is approximately the length of a football field. It takes just seconds to run.
13.	pole vault	An athlete jumps over a high bar by using a pole to lift himself or herself into the air.
14.	high jump	An athlete has three chances to make his or her highest jump.
15.	1500 m run	This is the final event of the second day. The race is a little less than a mile.
16.	shot put	An athlete throws a 16-pound metal ball as far as possible.
17.	110 m hurdles	While running, an athlete jumps over ten hurdles that are three-and-a-half feet tall.
18.	javelin throw	An athlete throws a special spear as far as possible.
19.	long jump	The longest jump out of three attempts is used.
20.	400 m run	This race is the final event of the first day.

STOP

Reading
2.5

Filling Out Applications

DIRECTIONS: Read the following application and fill in the information required.

Winston County Library Card Application

Patrons younger than 18 years old may be issued a library card if their parent or guardian's signature is on the library card application. Library cards are free to applicants who reside within the State of California. Library cards must be renewed every two years.

PLEASE PRINT

NAME: _____*Liang*_____ , _____*Jenna*_____ _____*Jia*_____
Last Name　　　　　　　First Name　　　　　　　Middle Name

ADDRESS: _____*Cypress St*_____ _____*25*_____
Street　　　　　　　　　　　　　　　　　　　Apt

_____*Vancouver*_____ _____*V6J 3M9*_____
City　　　　　　　　　　　　　　　　　　　Zip Code

TELEPHONE: Home (*604*) *634* *1685*

WINSTON COUNTY LIBRARY LENDING POLICY

Most circulating books may be borrowed for 28 days. Audiocassettes and videocassettes may be checked out for 7 days. Overdue items will be charged to the account of the cardholder at the rate of 10 cents per day for books, and $1.00 per day for audio and videocassettes.

BIRTHDATE IF UNDER 18: _____*August 24, 1998*_____

I agree to take responsibility for all materials borrowed on my library card, for their timely return, and for all charges incurred. I agree to notify the library immediately if the card is lost or stolen. I also agree to promptly advise the library of any changes in address, telephone number, or name.

SIGNATURE OF APPLICANT: _____*JIa*_____

DIRECTIONS: Answer the following questions.

1. **What is the cost of obtaining a library card?**

   _____*free*_____

2. **What is required for a person under age 18 to be issued a library card?**

   _____*Have their parent/guardian sihgn it.*_____

3. **How much is the fine for overdue videocassettes?**

   _____*$1:00*_____

   For overdue books?

   _____*10¢*_____

4. **How often must the library card be renewed?**

   _____*2 years*_____

2.6

Analyzing an Author's Evidence

The Sequoia

One natural wonder of the world is among the oldest and largest living things on Earth. It is the sequoia, a tree that once grew in plentiful varieties in forests over much of the world. Today, sequoias are found mainly in California. California is the only place where the two kinds of true sequoias—the redwood and the giant sequoia—still grow.

The redwood is the tallest living tree. It is found in the coastal mountains of northern California and southern Oregon. Growing in this warm, moist climate, the redwoods reach over 300 feet high. That's as tall as a 30-story building! The trunks of redwood trees are often more than 10 feet in diameter. The bark can be as thick as 12 inches. The redwood gets its name from the color of its wood, which turns from light to dark red as it weathers. Redwoods are sometimes called "California redwoods" or "coasts" since they grow along the Pacific coast of California.

The other true sequoia is the giant sequoia, which grows only on the western slopes of the Sierra Nevada Mountains in California. Once, the giant sequoias grew in many parts of the Northern Hemisphere. Today, they are found in only 70 groves. These giant sequoia groves are high in the mountains at elevations of 5,000 to 7,800 feet. Although giant sequoias do not grow as tall as redwoods, their trunks are much larger. Some trunks are as large as 100 feet around the base.

The largest tree in the world is found in Sequoia National Park. Named the General Sherman Tree, it stands 272.4 feet high and measures 101.6 feet around its base. Scientists believe that this single tree could produce over 600,000 board feet of lumber!

The giant sequoia is classified as an evergreen tree. It grows scale-like needles up to one-half inch long and produces woody oval-shaped cones about two to three inches long. Although lightning has destroyed the tops of many of the trees, they are considered to be among the hardiest of living things.

Scientists have dated many giant sequoias to be several thousand years old. The age is determined by counting the growth rings on a tree's trunk. Each growth ring stands for one year. Scientists have estimated that the General

Sherman Tree is at least 3,500 years old, and so it becomes not only the world's largest tree, but also one of the oldest living things on Earth.

Name _____ Date _____

DIRECTIONS: Fill in the blanks with information from the passage on page 23. See if you can guess how the author feels about the sequoia tree from these facts.

1. The giant sequoia once grew in many parts of the _____nothern_____ Hemisphere.

2. Today, the giant sequoia is found in only _____western_____ groves high in the mountains at elevations of

   _____5,000_____ to

   _____7,800_____ feet.

3. Sequoias are found mainly in

   _____California_____, where

   only _____true sequoias_____ kinds still

   grow: _____Redwoods_____ and

   _____Giant Sequoias_____.

4. The author of this passage is most likely to support which of the following?

   Ⓐ producing 600,000 board feet of lumber from the General Sherman Tree

   Ⓑ studying redwood trees instead of sequoias

   Ⓒ encouraging people to visit Sequoia National Park

   Ⓓ allowing lightning to burn down the tops of trees

5. Summarize in two or three sentences the author's purpose in writing about sequoia trees in this passage.

   _____Sequoias are_____
   _____wonderful trees._____
   _____They should be preserved_____
   _____for years to come_____

Making Assertions

Save the Elephants

Elephants are peaceful and magnificent animals. They live in social groups similar to families, with one female elephant, called a *matriarch,* leading the herd. As one of the largest land mammals in the world, African elephants have few predators. In fact, one of the greatest dangers to elephants in past years has not been from another animal, but from humans. The value of the ivory tusks on the elephants was irresistible to greedy hunters.

African elephants that live on the grassy savannah have long, curved tusks. Some African elephants live in forest areas. They have shorter tusks, allowing them to move more freely through the crowded forest. Both male and female elephants have tusks, which they use as a tool. Elephants tend to prefer either a right or left tusk, just as we favor our right or left hand. The tusk they use most often becomes shorter.

During the 1980s, the African elephant population was a casualty of human desires. The number of elephants declined from well over 1 million to about 600,000. It is estimated that more than 270 elephants were killed each day! Thousands of baby elephants, called *calves*, were left to take care of themselves. The African elephant was in a dangerous situation.

What was happening to the elephants? Poachers who wanted their ivory tusks were killing them. In many poor countries, poaching was one of the few ways to earn money. The ivory was valued around the world. It has been used for jewelry, statues, knife handles, billiard balls, piano keys, plus other products.

Organizations that protect animals and look out for their welfare were outraged. They devised a plan to alleviate the situation. They began a publicity campaign to spread awareness of the problem. Some large companies helped by refusing to buy ivory and asking their customers to do the same.

International laws were eventually passed to help make the killing of elephants less appealing. The sale of ivory was made illegal all around the world.

In recent days, "paintings" made by elephants have been used to raise money for elephant protection. Elephants use their trunks to hold the paintbrush. The paintings are then sold, with the money going toward conservation efforts.

GO

DIRECTIONS: Answer the following questions based on what you learned from the story on page 25.

1. **What could you learn about elephants by looking at their tusks?**

   That they use the shorter tusk more.

2. **What do you think would have happened to the African elephant if no one had made any changes?**

   I would think the elephants would almost be extinced.

3. **What is a poacher?**

   A poacher is a hunter but hunts illegaly.

4. **How do you think poachers were affected when ivory trade became illegal?**

   I think that it would be harder to smuggle the tusk and make money.

5. **What might happen to elephants if ivory trade was made legal again?**

   The elephant number would go down.

6. **What is the best way to continue to protect the elephants?**

   To help arrest poachers.

STOP

Analyzing Text

Hi-Yo, Silver!

What did people do for entertainment before television? Today, the average child spends more time watching television than reading. Television is so much a part of daily life that many people cannot imagine what life was like before it.

Before television, there was radio. Radio was invented around 1916 from the telegraph. At first, it was used to get information quickly from one part of the country to another. By 1926, radios were common in homes. People listened to music, news, and shows in the same way we watch TV today.

Television was not invented until the 1940s, and it did not gain popularity in homes until 1955. Families gathered around their radios to listen to shows broadcast all over the world. One of the most popular radio shows was *The Lone Ranger*. This show was about a Texas Ranger and a faithful Native American, named Tonto, who tirelessly worked to stop evil.

The Lone Ranger rode a white horse named Silver and wore a black mask. The Lone Ranger hid his identity, because a gang that ambushed and killed five other Texas Rangers had left him for dead. He vowed to find these desperadoes. His white hat, white horse, black mask, and his famous call, "Hi-yo, Silver. Away!" became symbols of the American Wild West hero.

Other famous radio heroes were the Shadow and the Green Hornet. Eventually, radio shows became famous television shows as well. Comedians and vaudeville stars made the transition from the stage to radio to television. Comedians such as Jack Benny, Red Skelton, and George Burns had radio shows that became television favorites.

GO

Name _____ Date _____

DIRECTIONS: Read the passage on page 27 and
answer the questions.

1. **What title best gives the main idea of this
   passage?**
   - (A) *The Lone Ranger Rides Again*
   - (B) *Before Television Came Radio*
   - (C) *Radio Stars Hit It Big on TV*
   - (D) *The History of Radio*

2. **What is not true of the passage?**
   - (F) It gives a brief history of radio.
   - (G) It tells about the transition from radio to
     television.
   - (H) It focuses on *The Lone Ranger* show.
   - (J) It shows how radio was far more
     popular than television.

3. **Which sentence below is an opinion?**
   - (A) *The Lone Ranger* was the best radio
     show ever.
   - (B) The Lone Ranger wore a white hat and
     black mask.
   - (C) Tonto was the Lone Ranger's faithful
     companion.
   - (D) *The Lone Ranger* took place in the
     American West.

4. **Which statement is true?**
   - (F) Tonto rode a white horse named Silver.
   - (G) Radio was invented in 1926.
   - (H) Several radio shows later became
     popular TV shows.
   - (J) Radio stars could not make it as
     television stars.

5. **Why do you suppose that *The Lone Ranger*
   was such a popular radio show?**
   - (A) Families had nothing better to do with
     their free time.
   - (B) It had the classic good guy against bad
     guys theme.
   - (C) People liked the special effects.
   - (D) People liked to watch the Lone Ranger
     and Tonto ride their horses.

6. **Why did the Lone Ranger wear a mask?**
   - (F) He wanted to hide his true identity.
   - (G) It was part of the Texas Ranger uniform.
   - (H) To shield his eyes from the sun.
   - (J) He wanted to be like his friend Tonto.

28

Reading

2.0

For pages 14–28

Mini-Test 2

DIRECTIONS: Read the following story and answer the questions.

Daedalus

According to a Greek myth, Daedalus was an inventor who had a son named Icarus. Daedalus designed the labyrinth, a maze of complicated passages that is very difficult to escape. Minos, the king of the island Crete, used the labyrinth to hide a monster called Minotaur, who was half man and half bull.

Daedalus did something to anger Minos, and the king made Daedalus and Icarus prisoners in the labyrinth. One day, Daedalus got an idea as he was watching birds fly. He asked Icarus to gather up all the bird feathers he could find. Then, using the feathers and some wax, Daedalus created two large pairs of wings. Soon he and Icarus were on their way over the walls of the labyrinth.

DIRECTIONS: Read the following events and answer question 1.

Q. Minos hid the Minotaur in the labyrinth.

R. Daedalus made Minos angry.

S. _____ .

T. Daedalus watched birds flying.

U. Daedalus and Icarus escaped.

1. **Which event is missing between R and T?**
   - (A) Icarus melted wax.
   - (B) Daedalus went to Crete.
   - (C) Icarus collected feathers.
   - (D) Daedalus and Icarus were imprisoned.

2. **Which of the following best describes Icarus?**
   - (F) a Greek prince
   - (G) a supernatural creature
   - (H) a rebellious child
   - (J) an innocent captive

3. **Which of the following was most likely the source of Daedalus's ideas for inventions?**
   - (A) Greek architecture
   - (B) the world of nature
   - (C) books and drawings
   - (D) the suggestions of King Minos

STOP

Reading Standards

3.0 Literary Response and Analysis

Students read and respond to historically or culturally significant works of literature that reflect and enhance their studies of history and social science. They clarify the ideas and connect them to other literary works.

Structural Features of Literature

3.1 Identify the forms of fiction and describe the major characteristics of each form. *(See page 31.)*

What it means:
- Forms of fiction include novels, poetry, legends, myths, and folktales. The term *genre* often is used to refer to these different types of literary compositions.

Narrative Analysis of Grade-Level-Appropriate Text

3.2 Analyze the effect of the qualities of the character (e.g., courage or cowardice, ambition or laziness) on the plot and the resolution of the conflict. *(See pages 32–33.)*

3.3 Analyze the influence of setting on the problem and its resolution. *(See pages 34–35.)*

3.4 Define how tone or meaning is conveyed in poetry through word choice, figurative language, sentence structure, line length, punctuation, rhythm, repetition, and rhyme. *(See page 36.)*

3.5 Identify the speaker and recognize the difference between first-and third-person narration (e.g., autobiography compared with biography). *(See page 37.)*

What it means:
- In a first-person narration, the author describes his or her own actions, emotions, or thoughts. In a third-person narration, the author describes someone else's actions, emotions, or thoughts.

3.6 Identify and analyze features of themes conveyed through characters, actions, and images. *(See page 38.)*

3.7 Explain the effects of common literary devices (e.g., symbolism, imagery, metaphor) in a variety of fictional and nonfictional texts. *(See pages 39–40.)*

Literary Criticism

3.8 Critique the credibility of characterization and the degree to which a plot is contrived or realistic (e.g., compare use of fact and fantasy in historical fiction). *(See page 41.)*

Reading
3.1

Identifying Forms of Fiction

Literary Response
and Analysis

DIRECTIONS: Identify the genre of each passage below.

1. **Act IV**

   Timothy enters his apartment and finds the furniture overturned, things thrown from the drawers. He picks up the telephone and dials 9-1-1.

   TIMOTHY: (fearfully) Yes, I need to report a break-in!! (pause) No, I haven't searched the entire apartment. (pause) Do you really think they could still be here?!

   _____

2. **The children awoke to a happy sight.**

   While they were sleeping, the world had turned white.

   Their mother peered into their room and said, "No school today. Go back to bed!

   _____

3. **Raccoon sat on the beach eating his potato. Before each bite he dipped the potato into the water. Monkey watched him from his perch in the tree and wondered about this curious habit.**

   _____

4. **The Himalayas are sometimes called the tallest mountains on earth. The truth is that several underwater ranges are even higher.**

   A passage like this would most likely be found in a book of—

   Ⓕ fables

   Ⓖ facts

   Ⓗ tall tales

   Ⓙ adventure stories

DIRECTIONS: Identify the genre of each title below.

5. *King Arthur and the Blazing Sword*

   Ⓐ nonfiction

   Ⓑ fable

   Ⓒ legend

   Ⓓ poetry

6. *All About Venus*

   Ⓕ nonfiction

   Ⓖ play

   Ⓗ legend

   Ⓙ folktale

7. *"Ode to an Owl, the Wisest of Fowl"*

   Ⓐ nonfiction

   Ⓑ legend

   Ⓒ fable

   Ⓓ poetry

8. *How Zebra Got His Stripes*

   Ⓕ legend

   Ⓖ folktale

   Ⓗ poetry

   Ⓙ play

STOP

Analyzing Characters

Slumber Party

It was the night Annabel had looked forward to for weeks. Four girls were arriving for a sleepover party! She had asked her parents many times, and finally they said yes. Annabel nervously wandered around the house, waiting for her guests to arrive. Finally, four cars pulled up and the doorbell rang.

Annabel threw open the door and welcomed her guests. The girls piled into Annabel's house in a jumble of sleeping bags and overnight cases.

"Thank you for inviting me," Robin said. "I brought you a thank-you gift." She held a small box out to her hostess.

"Yum! Chocolates!" Sheila shouted. She grabbed the box and shoved a candy into her mouth. She dropped the empty wrapper on the floor. "Got any milk?" she said, with her mouth full.

"There's milk in the kitchen," Annabel said as she pointed the way. Then, she noticed that another one of her guests did not look happy. "Tamiko, what's wrong?"

"I've never slept away from home," Tamiko admitted. "I'm a little nervous. My mother said I could call home if I needed to."

"You'll be all right," Annabel reassured her. "But, you can use the phone anytime. It's right over there . . . hey? Where's the phone?" She looked at the empty table. Her eyes followed the telephone cord to a corner of the room. A girl was talking animatedly into the phone. It was the last guest, Paula.

"Is it okay if my friend Dan comes over?" Paula called over to Annabel. "He says he's bored."

"No!" Annabel responded, a little shocked. "There are no boys at this slumber party. Well, except for my kid brother, Ted."

"Oh." Paula rolled her eyes and went back to chatting on the phone.

"I brought a flashlight and a teddy bear," Tamiko showed the girls. "They'll help me feel better in the middle of the night."

"I'll put my sleeping bag next to yours," Robin told her. "I hope that makes you feel safer."

"Don't worry," Annabel smiled. "There's nothing to be afraid of!"

"Oh, yeah?" Ted chuckled to himself from his hiding place at the top of the staircase. Annabel's brother was wearing a horrible monster mask, and he carried a plastic ax. "Just wait until I jump into their room at midnight!"

GO

Name _____ Date _____

DIRECTIONS: Read the story, then pick a word from the Word Bank to describe each of the characters. Write two examples from the story that prove why your description fits each person.

Word Bank		
fearful	greedy	polite
gracious	mischievous	rude

Example:

Annabel is <u>gracious</u>.
- A. She says "Welcome!" to her guests.
- B. She shows her friends where the milk and the phone are when she's asked.

1. Robin is _____.

A. _____

_____

B. _____

_____

2. Sheila is _____.

A. _____

_____

B. _____

_____

3. Tamiko is _____.

A. _____

_____

B. _____

_____

4. Paula is _____.

A. _____

_____

B. _____

_____

5. Ted is _____.

A. _____

_____

B. _____

_____

STOP

Analyzing the Influence of the Setting

Summer Camp

Our camp is great. A bunch of kids from school go there, but I especially like meeting kids from other schools. We sing crazy songs in the dining hall every noon. There are activities and challenges to try all day long. The counselors are great, the buildings are clean and airy, and the food is better than some meals I eat at home.

This year, Keesha is my counselor. She is so funny! She gets all us girls rolling on the cabin floor laughing at her silly, scary stories at bedtime. But she is smart, too. She knows when one of us is homesick or feels bad. She never pokes fun at us when we do something stupid. And she shows us how to express kindness to the others in our cabin. Keesha loves nature. She often points out the wildlife in camp. On our second morning of camp, Keesha raced outside as if there were a bee down her back. She yelled something about the witching hour. I always thought that the witching hour was at midnight. We all thought she had gone off the deep end. Keesha rushed over to a beech tree. The elephant-like trunk had a big hole in it where a woodpecker had hammered out a home. Our counselor reached her hands into the hole and pulled out a young possum. It chittered and squeaked until it saw us. Then it pretended to be asleep!

One night, she took all ten of us for a hike through the woods. She warned us to be quiet and to leave our flashlights at the cabin. We walked for twenty minutes when we stopped suddenly. We heard chattering creatures off to our right. Down by the lake, two raccoons were fighting over some bread. They sounded like two children squabbling over a treat.

One rainy day, we chose to go deep into the state forest with binoculars, guidebooks, insect repellent, and snack food. We sketched some of the wonderful flowering plants. Keesha knew the history and medicinal value of many of these plants. She showed us one plant that, when broken open, gave off a very powerful smell. She told us it would keep flies and mosquitoes away. I sure understood why the plant would work!

Every evening after supper, we'd play games with a group of kids from other cabins. Keesha volunteered me and my bunkmates to set up the evening game on our fifth day. We walked all over the camp, setting clues for a treasure hunt. This meant that we had to canoe to different landmarks around the lake, crawl under some of the older cabins, plan obscure hiding spots "that everyone should have known about," and race down the camp trails. Of course, we ran out of time. When the bell rang for supper, we were still far across the field.

In our giggle-filled dash to the dining hall, we waded through some tall grass. My new friend, Rita, unknowingly stepped over a light blue-gray snake. It was huge! Keesha said it was a blue racer. We all stood back and watched it, talking quietly. "Look how long it is," said Keesha. "It must be as long as I am!" We watched as the startled snake started to move slowly past us and then suddenly raced away. We were late for supper that day, but it didn't matter.

I want to go back to camp next summer. I want to know as much about nature as Keesha does. I can dream, can't I?

GO ➡

Name _____ Date _____

DIRECTIONS: Answer the following questions about the story "Summer Camp."

1. **List the two main elements of the setting.**

   Time: _____

   Place: _____

2. **Match the specific setting elements with these events by drawing lines to connect.**

EVENT	PLACE	TIME
see baby possum	in field	every noon
sing songs	by beech tree	rainy day
discover blue racer	in woods	bedtime
sketch plant specimens	in dining hall	second day
hear scary stories	in state forest	one night
observe raccoons	in cabin	fifth day

3. **Describe the summer camp by discussing the various activities of the campers.**

_____

_____

_____

_____

_____

_____

_____

_____

_____

_____

_____

_____

Understanding Tone and Meaning

A Doomed Romance

You are my love, my love you are.
I worship you from afar;
I through the branches spy you.
You, Sir, are a climbing thug.
I do not like your fuzzy mug.
Away from me, please take you!
Oh, grant me peace, my love, my dove.
Climb to my home so far above
This place you call your warren.
I like my home in sheltered hollow
Where fox and weasel may not follow.
Please go away, tree rodent!

I love your ears, so soft and tall.
I love your nose, so pink and small.
I must make you my own bride!
I will not climb, I cannot eat
The acorns that you call a treat.
Now shimmy up that oak; hide!
Now I hide up in my bower.
Lonesome still, I shake and cower.
Sadness overtakes me.
I must stay on the lovely ground
With carrots crisp and cabbage round.
I long for gardens, not trees.

DIRECTIONS: Answer the following questions about the poem.

1. **Who are the two speakers in this ballad? Identify them and write one adjective to describe the tone of each voice.**

    A. _____

    _____

    B. _____

    _____

2. **Briefly, what story does the poem tell? Explain in one complete sentence.**

    _____

    _____

    _____

    _____

    _____

    _____

3. **What do you think the theme of this poem is? Write it in one phrase or sentence.**

    _____

    _____

    _____

    _____

    _____

4. **Circle two adjectives to describe the first speaker in the poem.**

    angry   lovesick

    happy   hopeful   silly

5. **Circle two adjectives to describe the second speaker in the poem.**

    joyful   relaxed

    annoyed   realistic   happy

STOP

Reading
3.5

Identifying Point of View

Literary Response
and Analysis

DIRECTIONS: Below are 10 short paragraphs. In each blank, write **1** for first person, **2** for second person, or **3** for third person to identify the point of view of each.

Example:

_____ Your heart is thumping in your chest as the car slowly makes its way to the top of the hill. You risk looking down just as the roller coaster reaches the very top and begins its mad drop.

Answer: 2

1. _____ It's true, you know? You always loved cats more than people. When you first saw . . . what was that cat's name? Oh, yes, Bernard! When your dad brought Bernard home from the shelter, you looked like you had gone to heaven and seen an angel.

2. _____ A domestic turkey is not a wise bird. A dog, fox, or weasel that finds its way into a turkey coop merely waits for some lamebrained and curious turkey to waddle over for a visit. The predator has a cooperative victim!

3. _____ I don't think I can stand it any longer. I've got to tell Mom how much I dislike her asparagus custard pie. But how do I do it without hurting her feelings?

4. _____ That stubborn bachelor Patches McCloud had better get out of his termite-infested apartment before the walls come tumbling in on him! No one need warn him again!

5. _____ When you were born, the sun smiled down upon the earth. The moon glowed. The creatures of the night forest whispered that you, a princess, had been born to our people.

6. _____ What? You—become an army sharpshooter? Why, you couldn't hit the broad side of a barn if you were leaning against it!

7. _____ She carried a large basket of laundry on her head. She had done chores like this since she was a tiny child. But this time, things were different. Mikela was working at a real job now. Wouldn't her mother be proud!

8. _____ Oh, it was so dark! We will never know what caused the sudden blackout at the ball game. We hope the game will be rescheduled.

9. _____ The song "Yankee Doodle" was used by British soldiers to mock the colonials who opposed them. But the colonists were smart enough to realize that if they embraced the mockery, it would take the sting out of it. So, the song became their anthem.

10. _____ It's backbreaking work. All day long, we are bent over at the waist as we carefully replant our rice in the flooded paddy. But our feet tingle in the cool, rich, oozing mud.

Reading

Identifying and Analyzing Themes

The Race Is On!

Lee and Kim are both running for class president. This is a big job. The president has to help organize special events for the class, such as environmental projects, holiday parties, visit-the-elderly outings, and field trips. Lee has been campaigning for several weeks. He really wants to be elected president. He prepared a speech telling the class all of the great ideas he hopes to accomplish if he wins. For example, Lee wants to have a car wash and picnic to earn money for the homeless. He also wants to recycle aluminum cans to earn money for a field trip to the new Exploration Science Center. Lee has been working hard for this position.

Kim hasn't done much, if any, campaigning. She figures she has lots of friends who will vote for her. Instead of a speech, she gave a big pool party at her house. Kim believes the class should work to earn money, but she believes that any money they raise should be used for their class. Why give money to someone else when there are lots of great places to visit on field trips in their city? The day of the big election arrives. The votes are in. The winner is . . .

DIRECTIONS: Answer the questions below using information from the story.

1. **What kind of person is Lee? How do you know?**

   _____

   _____

   _____

2. **What kind of person is Kim? How do you know?**

   _____

   _____

   _____

3. **Who do you think will win the election? Why?**

   _____

   _____

   _____

4. **If Lee is the winner, what is the theme of this story?**

   _____

   _____

   _____

   _____

   _____

5. **If Kim is the winner, what is the theme of this story?**

   _____

   _____

   _____

   _____

Understanding
Literary Devices

The Escape

Into the shady glen the small figure rode on a pony little larger than a dog. The pony's breath misted in the crisp air as the beast blew air out of its nostrils. The green-mantled figure patted the neck of the beast, whispering words of comfort into the animal's ear. In response, the faithful steed nickered, thumped his wide hoofs twice upon the soft bed of the forest floor, and ceased its shaking.

"We've left the raiders behind, old friend," said Rowan, as she removed her hooded mantle and tossed her head back and forth, bringing peace to her own troubled mind. Rowan was one of four daughters of Sylvia, guide of all wood folk.

Suddenly, shouts of rough men cut through the glade's peace.

"In here, I tell ya. The maid's gone to hiding in this grove." "Nah, ya lunk. She'd never wait for us here. Not after she dunked old Stefan at the marsh. No! She's a gone on to her crazy folk, don'tcha know."

The two gray-cloaked riders dismounted, still arguing as they examined the earth for traces of the child's flight.

"Who was the lout who let her escape?" asked the first.

"'Tis one who no longer breathes the air so freely," returned the second grimly. "The lord nearly choked the fool, even as the knave begged for mercy. Ah, there's little patience for one who lets a mystic escape, to be true!"

Five nobly dressed horsemen wove through the trees to the clearing where these two rustics still squatted. In the lead came the fierce lord, a huge form with scarlet and gray finery worn over his coat of mail.

"What say you?" he roared. "Have you found the trail of Rowan?"

"No, sire," spoke the first gray, trembling, "though I was certain the child headed into this wood. Shall I continue to search, lord?"

"Aye, indeed," replied the master calmly, controlled. "She is here. I know it, too. You have a keen sense for the hunt, Mikkel. Be at ready with your blade. And you too, Short Brush! Though a child, our Rowan is vicious with her weapon."

"Yes, sire," agreed Mikkel and Short Brush.

The two grays beat the bushes in the search. Closer and closer they came to the child's hiding place, a small earthen scoop created when the roots of a wind-blown tree pulled free of the earth.

The evil lord and his lot remained mounted, ready to pursue should the young girl determine to take flight once more. And so, they were not prepared for the child's play.

Rowan softly, softly sang, "You wind-whipped branches shudder, shake. You oaks and cedars, tremble. Take these men and beasts who do us wrong. Not in these woods do they belong."

As a mighty gust of wind roared, nearby trees slapped their branches to the point of breaking, reaching out and grasping the five mounted men. An immense gaping cavern opened in the trunk of an ancient oak and swallowed the five surprised mail-clad men whole.

Mikkel and Short Brush, too, were lifted high into the air by a white pine and a blue spruce. Lifted high. Kept high. For a while.

"Return from whence you came. Go to your families, and tell them of the wrath of Sylvia," commanded Rowan. "She would not wish you to come to her land again!"

The pine and spruce tossed the two gray trackers over the trees of the forest and into the field beyond. The field was already harvested and soggy with the rains of autumn. Mikkel and Short Brush, unhurt but shaken by their arboreal flight, rose and fled immediately to tell their master of the strange doings of this wood.

GO

Name _____ Date _____

DIRECTIONS: Read the story on page 39, then answer the questions.

1. **What details tell the reader that Rowan is very small?**

_____

_____

_____

_____

_____

2. **What details help you picture the fierce lord?**

_____

_____

_____

_____

_____

3. **What details convey that Rowan is in great danger if caught?**

_____

_____

_____

_____

_____

4. **Draw a sketch of your idea of what the oak tree swallowing the five horsemen looks like.**

Reading

3.8

Literary Response and Analysis

Identifying Realistic Plots

 Clue   Remember that a contrived plot is one in which the conflict is wrapped up too easily or with a very unlikely coincidence.

DIRECTIONS: Choose the answer below that would be the most contrived, or least realistic, plot for the story that is described.

1. **Jack and Andrew are hopelessly lost in the desert. They have run out of food and have only a little water. After two nights of walking, they _____ .**

   (A) happen upon a group of nomads who care for them

   (B) find an oasis with water, dried food, and an abandoned satellite phone

   (C) find a stray camel who carries them to civilization

   (D) are awakened by the sound of the search party's helicopter

2. **Jayda leaves home determined to make it as an actress in New York. She auditions for many plays but is not offered any parts. Finally she is down to her last $10. She then _____ .**

   (F) finds a job as a waitress and enrolls in acting lessons

   (G) meets a man who is directing a play and needs an actress for the starring role

   (H) decides to move to Hollywood instead

   (J) calls her parents to bring her home and abandons her hopes of stardom

3. **The crop has failed for the second year in a row. The bank is about to take the farm. Then, one day _____ .**

   (A) Jacob is hoeing in the field and strikes oil. The family is rich beyond imagination!

   (B) Aunt Matilda's will, which has been missing for a year, is found in a book. She has left the family enough money to pay off their debts.

   (C) the entire community comes together to donate enough money for the family to keep the farm

   (D) Jacob begs the bank manger to give him one last chance to pay his debts, and the manager agrees to wait one more year.

Name _____   Date _____

Reading

3.0

For pages 31–41

Literary Response
and Analysis

Mini-Test 3

DIRECTIONS: Write the letter in the blank that matches each of the qualities on the left with the quotation on the right.

1. _____ hot-tempered

2. _____ embarrassed

3. _____ confused

4. _____ tired

5. _____ sneaky

6. _____ clumsy

7. _____ ecstatic

8. _____ accusatory

9. _____ foolish

10. _____ melancholy

11. _____ obnoxious

12. _____ spendthrift

13. _____ crabby

A. "Hey, let's try to run across that busy street," suggested Stan.

B. "I don't think I can walk another step," sighed Sanders, falling into a nearby recliner.

C. Wrinkling his face, Sean frowned, "You can't make me finish my work!"

D. "Shh! Get your head down, Sarah. Don't let Mrs. Lions see us," whispered Wanda.

E. "Oops! I'm sorry. I thought you were my brother," moaned Martha as she wiped ketchup off the waiter's white shirt.

F. "Uhhh. Four . . . no, seven . . .Uhh. Is this true or false, Miss Jacobs?" inquired Isaac.

G. "No, just go ahead to the movie without me. I think I'll just stay home and cry myself to sleep," croaked Craig.

H. "Oh, how wonderful! My very own Darby Delight Dollhouse!" squealed Skeeter.

I. "Hey, I just stepped on your feet. Oops! I did it again!" giggled Garth.

J. "Aww come on, Ron! You must have eaten that blueberry pie. You've got crumbs on your chin and a stain on your shirt," observed Oscar.

K. "Leave me alone! Just get out of my face!" shouted Sheri.

L. "Hey there's another penny! That makes 42 cents I've saved this week," muttered Mindy.

M. "What a dump! Hey string bean! Get over here and take my order," demanded Damion.

How Am I Doing?

Mini-Test 1

Page 12

Number Correct

13–16 answers correct	**Great Job!** Move on to the section test on page 44.
8–12 answers correct	**You're almost there!** But you still need a little practice. Review practice pages 8–11 before moving on to the section test on page 44.
0–7 answers correct	**Oops!** Time to review what you have learned and try again. Review the practice section on pages 8–11. Then retake the test on page 12. Now move on to the section test on page 44.

Mini-Test 2

Page 29

Number Correct

3 answers correct	**Awesome!** Move on to the section test on page 44.
2 answers correct	**You're almost there!** But you still need a little practice. Review practice pages 14–28 before moving on to the section test on page 44.
0–1 answers correct	**Oops!** Time to review what you have learned and try again. Review the practice section on pages 14–28. Then retake the test on page 29. Now move on to the section test on page 44.

Mini-Test 3

Page 42

Number Correct

11–13 answers correct	**Great Job!** Move on to the section test on page 44.
8–10 answers correct	**You're almost there!** But you still need a little practice. Review practice pages 31–41 before moving on to the section test on page 44.
0–7 answers correct	**Oops!** Time to review what you have learned and try again. Review the practice section on pages 31–41. Then retake the test on page 42. Now move on to the section test on page 44.

Final Reading Test
for pages 8–42

DIRECTIONS: Choose the best answer.

1. **Which of the following is a simile?**
   - (A) The bread was not as soft as it should have been.
   - (B) The bread was left out and became stale.
   - (C) The bread was as hard as a rock.
   - (D) The bread was delicious with strawberry jam.

2. **Which of the following is a metaphor?**
   - (F) His harsh words were difficult for Dana to take.
   - (G) His words were hammers, pounding at Dana.
   - (H) Dana was upset by his harsh words.
   - (J) His harsh words made Dana's head pound.

DIRECTIONS: Choose the word that correctly completes both sentences.

3. **What's all that _____?**
   He hit the ball with his _____.
   - (A) noise
   - (B) bat
   - (C) commotion
   - (D) racket

4. **The stars _____ at night.**
   You _____ to be ill.
   - (F) seem
   - (G) pretend
   - (H) appear
   - (J) shine

DIRECTIONS: Read the passage, then choose the word that best fits each blank.

Laughter is good medicine. Scientists believe that laughter _____ (5) the heart and lungs. Laughter burns calories and may help _____ (6) blood pressure. It also _____ (7) stress and tension.
If you are _____ (8) about an upcoming test, laughter can help you relax.

5.
   - (A) heals
   - (B) stresses
   - (C) weakens
   - (D) strengthens

6.
   - (F) raise
   - (G) lower
   - (H) eliminate
   - (J) elongate

7.
   - (A) relieves
   - (B) increases
   - (C) revives
   - (D) releases

8.
   - (F) excited
   - (G) enthusiastic
   - (H) nervous
   - (J) knowledgeable

GO

DIRECTIONS: Read the passage, then answer the questions.

The practice of wearing rings is a very ancient one. Throughout history, people in many lands have decorated their bodies by wearing rings on their fingers, ears, lips, necks, noses, ankles, and wrists. In some cultures, a married woman wore a ring on the big toe of her left foot; a man might have put rings on his second and third toes. Today, the practice of wearing rings in some cases includes multiple facial rings, as well as rings in many other areas of the body.

9. **What is the paragraph mainly about?**
   - (A) why some people wore rings on their toes
   - (B) what kinds of rings were the most popular
   - (C) when the practice of wearing rings began
   - (D) how people throughout history have worn rings

10. **Which title best summarizes this passage?**
    - (F) "Rings Worn Today"
    - (G) "Rings Throughout the Ages"
    - (H) "Rings in Unusual Places"
    - (J) "Rings Are Fun"

DIRECTIONS: Read the letter, then answer the questions.

Dear Mrs. Brewton,

Aloha from the big island! This state is so beautiful! We had the chance to drive fairly close to the volcano again this week, and then we went to a great luau. I'm learning a lot about the land, people, and wildlife here. I never thought I'd see some of the rocks and plants you talked about in class.

I've met a few more kids this past week. I've made a lot of friends since school ended last month in June. By the way, how are things in North Country? Any news from those friendly Americans to your south? The kids here think we only play hockey and race dogsleds. They were stunned to find out I love to kick the old ball around. I don't get to play fullback or goalie as much as I do back home, but it's still good practice for being on the team again next fall.

11. **Where is the writer of the letter living this summer?**
    - (A) Canada
    - (B) Alaska
    - (C) Mexico
    - (D) Hawaii

12. **Where is the writer's home?**
    - (F) Canada
    - (G) Alaska
    - (H) Mexico
    - (J) Hawaii

13. **Who is Mrs. Brewton?**
    - (A) the writer's sister
    - (B) the writer's bus driver
    - (C) the writer's dentist
    - (D) the writer's teacher

14. **What type of sports team will the writer be on next fall?**
    - (F) soccer
    - (G) hockey
    - (H) dogsledding
    - (J) basketball

GO

DIRECTIONS: Read the passage below, then answer the questions.

As she walked along the sandy shore
with delight as nature's wonders she did see
starfish, whitecaps, conch shells, and more.
She knew that she would never fly free
like the tissue-paper seagulls above
or swim with the dolphins she did love.

15. What type of fiction is the passage above?

- (A) novel
- (B) poem
- (C) play
- (D) folktale

16. Which of the following is a metaphor?

- (F) the sandy shore
- (G) tissue-paper seagulls
- (H) she would never fly free
- (J) nature's wonders

DIRECTIONS: Read the following passage, then answer the questions.

One afternoon in March, I found two silver dollars shining in a half-melted snow bank. I instantly thought of buried treasure. So I dug through the snow searching for more. All I ended up with were two really cold hands. I slipped the two coins in my pocket and went home colder but richer.

The next morning, Megan and her little sister were searching the snow banks. "Finders keepers" was my first thought. I didn't need to get to the losers weepers part since Moira was already crying for real. "I dropped them right here," she said between tears. Her hands were red from digging in the snow. "Maybe they got shoved down the street by the snow plow. Let's try over there," Megan said optimistically.

"They'll never know" was my second thought, as I walked past them toward Tyler's house.

"Phil, have you seen two silver dollars?" Megan called. Moira looked up from the snow bank with hope bright in her eyes.

"Coins?" "Look innocent" was my third thought.

"Yes, Moira dropped two silver dollars somewhere around here yesterday." "Yeah," said Moira, "they're big and heavy." She brushed her icy red hands off on her jacket and wiped the tears from her eyes. Her eyes were as red as her hands.

I hesitated, but only for a moment. Then I said, "As a matter of fact, I dug two coins out of that snow bank yesterday. I wondered who might have lost them. Moira ran to me and gave me a bear hug. "Oh, thank you, thank you!" I couldn't help but smile.

17. The story is written from the _____ perspective.

- (A) first-person
- (B) second-person
- (C) third-person
- (D) None of these

18. What is the theme of this story?

- (F) It is okay to lie if you think you will get away with it.
- (G) It is always better to be honest than rich.
- (H) "Finders keepers, losers weepers" is not a good saying to live by.
- (J) Both G and H apply.

19. What is the setting of this story?

- (A) outside on a March day
- (B) outside on a warm, sunny day
- (C) inside on a rainy spring day
- (D) the view outside a window

20. Overall, what type of person is Phil?

   (F) ambitious and unfair

   (G) honest and caring

   (H) greedy and cruel

   (J) dishonest and angry

21. Which statement below is a fact?

   (A) Phil thinks only of his own wants.

   (B) Moira cries a lot.

   (C) Moira and Phil should be wearing mittens when out in the snow.

   (D) Moira is crying because she has lost her silver dollars.

22. What images from the story convey that Moira has been searching for the coins for a long time?

   (F) Moira is crying.

   (G) Moira says the coins are big and heavy.

   (H) Megan is optimistic.

   (J) Moira's hands are red and cold from digging.

23. How did Phil probably feel at the end of the story? He felt _____.

   (A) angry with himself for being honest

   (B) angry with Megan and Moira

   (C) hopeful that he would find another buried treasure

   (D) disappointed at having to give up the coins but glad that he had been honest

24. Which would be the most contrived ending?

   (F) Moira is so grateful she gives Phil one of the silver dollars.

   (G) Phil's parents praise him for being honest.

   (H) Phil never forgets that being honest is its own reward.

   (J) None of these is contrived.

STOP

Final Reading Test
Answer Sheet

1 Ⓐ Ⓑ Ⓒ Ⓓ
2 Ⓕ Ⓖ Ⓗ Ⓙ
3 Ⓐ Ⓑ Ⓒ Ⓓ
4 Ⓕ Ⓖ Ⓗ Ⓙ
5 Ⓐ Ⓑ Ⓒ Ⓓ
6 Ⓕ Ⓖ Ⓗ Ⓙ
7 Ⓐ Ⓑ Ⓒ Ⓓ
8 Ⓕ Ⓖ Ⓗ Ⓙ
9 Ⓐ Ⓑ Ⓒ Ⓓ
10 Ⓕ Ⓖ Ⓗ Ⓙ

11 Ⓐ Ⓑ Ⓒ Ⓓ
12 Ⓕ Ⓖ Ⓗ Ⓙ
13 Ⓐ Ⓑ Ⓒ Ⓓ
14 Ⓕ Ⓖ Ⓗ Ⓙ
15 Ⓐ Ⓑ Ⓒ Ⓓ
16 Ⓕ Ⓖ Ⓗ Ⓙ
17 Ⓐ Ⓑ Ⓒ Ⓓ
18 Ⓕ Ⓖ Ⓗ Ⓙ
19 Ⓐ Ⓑ Ⓒ Ⓓ
20 Ⓕ Ⓖ Ⓗ Ⓙ

21 Ⓐ Ⓑ Ⓒ Ⓓ
22 Ⓕ Ⓖ Ⓗ Ⓙ
23 Ⓐ Ⓑ Ⓒ Ⓓ
24 Ⓕ Ⓖ Ⓗ Ⓙ

Writing Standards

1.0 Writing Strategies

Students write clear, coherent, and focused essays. The writing exhibits students' awareness of the audience and purpose. Essays contain formal introductions, supporting evidence, and conclusions. Students progress through the stages of the writing process as needed.

Organization and Focus

1.1 Choose the form of writing (e.g., personal letter, letter to the editor, review, poem, report, narrative) that best suits the intended purpose. *(See page 50.)*

1.2 Create multiple-paragraph expository compositions:
   a. Engage the interest of the reader and state a clear purpose.
   b. Develop the topic with supporting details and precise verbs, nouns, and adjectives to paint a visual image in the mind of the reader.
   c. Conclude with a detailed summary linked to the purpose of the composition. *(See page 51.)*

1.3 Use a variety of effective and coherent organizational patterns, including comparison and contrast; organization by categories; and arrangement by spatial order, order of importance, or climactic order. *(See pages 52–53.)*

Research and Technology

1.4 Use organizational features of electronic text (e.g., bulletin boards, databases, keyword searches, e-mail addresses) to locate information.

1.5 Compose documents with appropriate formatting by using word-processing skills and principles of design (e.g., margins, tabs, spacing, columns, page orientation).

Evaluation and Revision

1.6 Revise writing to improve the organization and consistency of ideas within and between paragraphs. *(See page 54.)*

Linking Purpose to Writing

DIRECTIONS: Choose the form of writing that would best suit the author's stated purpose.

1. **The author wants to tell her aunt about her Science Fair project.**
   - (A) a personal letter
   - (B) a report
   - (C) a business letter
   - (D) a letter to the editor

2. **The author wants to encourage all citizens to vote for the school bond levy.**
   - (F) a personal letter
   - (G) a letter to the editor
   - (H) a report
   - (J) a review

3. **The author wants to share her feelings about a beautiful sunset.**
   - (A) a poem
   - (B) a letter to the editor
   - (C) a review
   - (D) a report

4. **The author wants to tell others about the special effects, script, and acting in a new science fiction movie he just watched.**
   - (F) a personal letter
   - (G) a review
   - (H) a poem
   - (J) a letter to the editor

5. **The author wants to apply for a position as summer camp counselor.**
   - (A) a poem
   - (B) a letter to the editor
   - (C) a business letter
   - (D) a personal letter

6. **The author wants to inform his classmates about the history of skateboarding.**
   - (F) a business letter
   - (G) a review
   - (H) a personal letter
   - (J) a report

7. **What is the purpose of the following passage?**

   The floor plan of a house determines how livable it is. The kitchen, for example, should be close to the dining room. Bedrooms are best located far from the kitchen or living room so they will be quiet.
   - (A) to entertain
   - (B) to persuade
   - (C) to inform
   - (D) None of these

8. **What is the purpose of the following passage?**

   If you want to get the most for your money you'll shop at Hedrick's Supermarket. We have the freshest meats and produce in the city. Our prices can't be beat!
   - (F) to entertain
   - (G) to persuade
   - (H) to inform
   - (J) None of these

9. **What is the purpose of the following passage?**

   The house was shrouded in darkness. Should we go in or wait for help to arrive?
   "It's now or never!" Sondra yelled, as she and Bart crashed through the door.
   - (A) to entertain
   - (B) to persuade
   - (C) to inform
   - (D) None of these

50

Writing

Writing Strategies

1.2

Writing to Explain

DIRECTIONS: Write a composition responding to the following question: Do you think there is too much violence on TV, in the movies, and in video games? Remember to clearly state your purpose for writing, develop your topic with supporting details, and conclude with a detailed summary.

I think there are too much violence in viedo games, t.v, and movies. There is too much blood and other stuff. The movies, t.v, and viedo games should be safer. I don't mean that there can be no action scenes, but the games are just to violent. Maybe in the future there might be violent free t.v, movies and viedo games for children.

Organizing Information

Going to the Dogs

Paws with a Cause (PAWS) is a nonprofit organization that provides specially trained "hearing" and "service" dogs to people with disabilities. It began in 1979 in Byron Center, Michigan, and was originally called Ears for the Deaf.

At first, the organization trained dogs to assist the hearing impaired. Over time, it expanded its training to include service dogs. A service dog allows a physically challenged person to have more independence. In addition, PAWS trains dogs to help individuals with multiple disabilities.

PAWS trainers select dogs from animal shelters and humane societies across the United States. Over 95 percent of the hearing dogs have been saved from possible death at these shelters. These dogs are then taken to the training center, where they spend several months in specific skill training.

The dogs' training consists of three parts. All the dogs are given basic obedience training. They learn to respond to commands such as "sit," "come," and "down." Dogs being trained for the hearing impaired are also given specific sound-alert training. These dogs learn to respond to six sounds: door knock, doorbell ring, two types of telephone rings, alarm clock, smoke alarm, and an intruder. Service dogs receive advanced training geared to the individual person's needs. They may learn how to turn off lights, pick up dropped objects, close doors, or serve as a support for walking. The third phase of training takes place at the recipient's home. A field trainer helps the dog bond with a new owner, learn commands, and get familiar with the needs and routines of the owner.

A trained dog is expensive. A hearing dog costs approximately $5,000. A service dog costs around $8,500. Individuals with disabilities may purchase the dogs with their own money. PAWS has an active donation fund to assist individuals with the expenses incurred, but the waiting period is lengthy. Some organizations sponsor walk-a-thons or other fund drives to raise money for a member of their community. Also, generous students have earned money through creative methods such as the "Read-a-Million-Minutes" program.

In addition to rescuing many dogs from animal shelters and then training them for specific service, PAWS spends a great deal of time educating the public. Through community awareness presentations, PAWS is helping the public understand the legal rights of hearing and service dogs and the ongoing need for these dogs. With the help of Paws with a Cause, having a disability does not mean living with an inability.

GO

Name _____ Date _____

DIRECTIONS: Complete the story map with details from the passage.

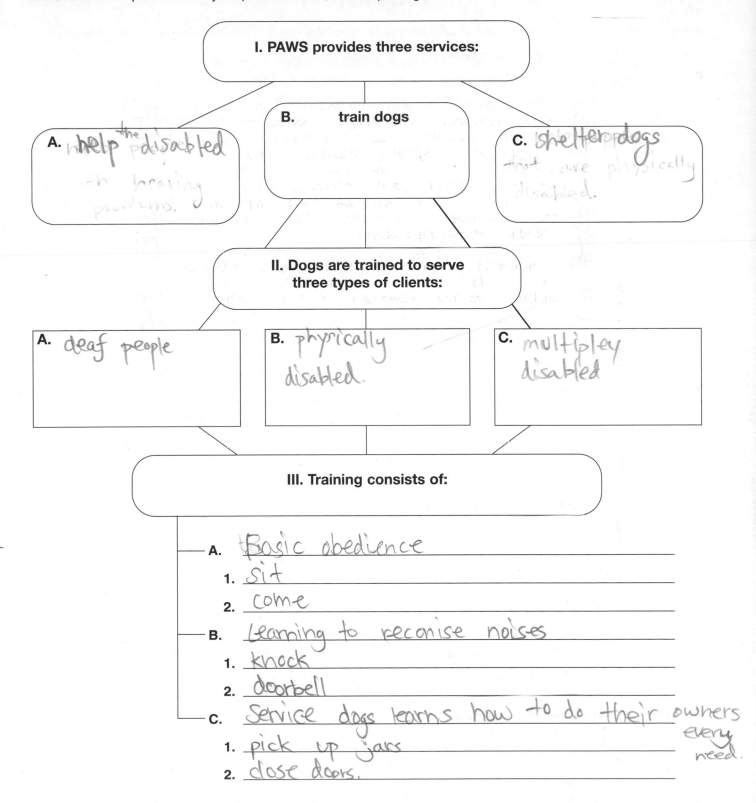

I. PAWS provides three services:

A. help the disabled with hearing problems.

B. train dogs

C. shelter dogs that are physically disabled.

II. Dogs are trained to serve three types of clients:

A. deaf people

B. physically disabled.

C. multipley disabled

III. Training consists of:

A. Basic obedience

   1. sit

   2. come

B. Learning to reconise noises

   1. knock

   2. doorbell

C. Service dogs learns how to do their owners every need.

   1. pick up jars

   2. close doors.

STOP

Revising

> (1) Kerry was always wary of his brother: listening for footsteps or watching for flying objects such as books, toys, or sticks. (2) Once it was a large platter of pancakes. (3) Kerry had to keep his eyes open. (4) He also had to keep his ears open at all times. (5) Although Kerry and Jimmy were only a year apart, the boys were as different as Laurel and Hardy or Fred and Barney. (6) Jimmy, the older brother, was in seventh grade and was already six-feet tall and weighed 180 pounds. (7) But his mom loved him and thought he was a good boy.
>
> (8) Jimmy was especially frightening today because he had a temper, which was large to match his size. (9) Today was the day of the annual race competition between the sixth and seventh graders. (10) The sixth graders were sure to win.
>
> (11) What Kerry lacked in size, he made up for in speed.
>
> (12) He was the fastest runner in the school. (13) And that was the problem. (14) Jimmy would be furious.

DIRECTIONS: Answer the questions based on the passage above.

1. How are sentences 3 and 4 best combined?

(A) Kerry had to keep his eyes open, and he had to keep his ears open at all times.

(B) At all times, Kerry had to keep open his eyes and his ears also.

(C) Kerry at all times had to keep his eyes open and his ears also.

(D) Kerry had to keep his eyes and ears open at all times.

2. Which sentence does not belong in this story?

(F) Sentence 2

(G) Sentence 7

(H) Sentence 8

(J) Sentence 14

3. How is sentence 8 best written?

(A) Jimmy had a temper to match his size, which made him especially frightening today.

(B) Like his large size, Jimmy's temper was also large today, which made him especially frightening.

(C) Jimmy had a large temper and a large size, which made him especially frightening today.

(D) Today Jimmy had a temper, which was large to match his size, and he was especially frightening.

Writing

1.0

For pages 50–54

Mini-Test 1

DIRECTIONS: Read the passage then answer the questions.

> **(1)** Years ago people believed that children could not write until they could spell. **(2)** Children practiced letters or were given spelling words or dictation to copy, but schools did not consider scribbling to be writing. **(3)** Children in early elementary school spent their time painting or playing with blocks or clay. **(4)** Scribbling then was just scribbling. **(5)** Teachers now believes, that encouraging young children to scribble is an important step in writing. **(6)** Teachers have discovered that it is important for children to write before they even know their alphabet. **(7)** Young children encouraged to write lists and tell stories, leave messages and make signs. **(8)** They should be asked to read their writing aloud, although unreadable it may be.

1. **Which sentence should be added after sentence 5?**

   (A) Recess was my favorite activity of the day.

   (B) This early writing may not be readable, but it is still writing.

   (C) Playing dress up and other play activities also are beneficial.

   (D) Naptime is a necessary part of the young child's day.

2. **How is sentence 8 best written?**

   (F) Even because it is unreadable, they should be asked to read their writing aloud.

   (G) They should be asked to read their writing aloud, even if it is unreadable.

   (H) Because they should be asked to read their unreadable writing aloud.

   (J) As it is

3. **Which group of words is not a complete thought?**

   (A) Sentence 2

   (B) Sentence 3

   (C) Sentence 7

   (D) Sentence 8

4. **In sentence 5, "believes, that encouraging" is best written —**

   (F) believe that encouraging

   (G) believe. That encouraging

   (H) believe that, encouraging

   (J) As it is

Writing Standards

2.0 Writing Applications (Genres and Their Characteristics)

Students write narrative, expository, persuasive, and descriptive texts of at least 500 to 700 words in each genre. Student writing demonstrates a command of standard American English and the research, organizational, and drafting strategies outlined in Writing Standard 1.0.

Using the writing strategies of grade six outlined in Writing Standard 1.0, students:

2.1 Write narratives:

  a. Establish and develop a plot and setting and present a point of view that is appropriate to the stories.

  b. Include sensory details and concrete language to develop plot and character.

  c. Use a range of narrative devices (e.g., dialogue, suspense). *(See page 57.)*

What it means:
- Narratives are stories or events that have a clear beginning, middle, and end.

2.2 Write expository compositions (e.g., description, explanation, comparison and contrast, problem and solution):

  a. State the thesis or purpose.

  b. Explain the situation.

  c. Follow an organizational pattern appropriate to the type of composition.

  d. Offer persuasive evidence to validate arguments and conclusions as needed. *(See page 58.)*

2.3 Write research reports:

  a. Pose relevant questions with a scope narrow enough to be thoroughly covered.

  b. Support the main idea or ideas with facts, details, examples, and explanations from multiple authoritative sources (e.g., speakers, periodicals, online information searches).

  c. Include a bibliography. *(See pages 59–60.)*

2.4 Write responses to literature:

  a. Develop an interpretation exhibiting careful reading, understanding, and insight.

  b. Organize the interpretation around several clear ideas, premises, or images.

  c. Develop and justify the interpretation through sustained use of examples and textual evidence. *(See page 61.)*

2.5 Write persuasive compositions:

  a. State a clear position on a proposition or proposal.

  b. Support the position with organized and relevant evidence.

  c. Anticipate and address reader concerns and counterarguments. *(See page 62.)*

Writing

2.1

Writing Narratives

DIRECTIONS: Write a short story. Decide on the plot, setting, and point of view. Remember to include sensory details to develop your characters.

A dark damp morning chilled people to the bone in Shatville. It especally chilled little Bob. Bob was tired of being called shrimp, he decided to go to the center of the earth. Little Bob went to machine shop bough a drill and dug slowly to the earth. Once he got out on the surface he was in China!. Bob thought at least it's warm and lived happily after ever.

THE END

Writing a Composition

DIRECTIONS: Write a 1-page composition on the following subject: How has the world changed because of cellular phones? Offer evidence to support your view.

Cell phones are great they provide easy communication without people writing letters. Now people use cells all the time. Sometimes if your in an emergancy just reach in your pocket grab your phone and call somebody.

Writing
2.3

Writing a Research Report

DIRECTIONS: Organize the following facts and write a short research report on the next page. Clearly state the main idea and support it with facts. Use only those details that are necessary to your main idea.

From an article "The Essential Amadeus" by Christopher Morrow in *Classical Music Magazine* vol. 34 (May 2002) p: 29–30.

Wolfgang Amadeus Mozart was born on January 27, 1756, in Salzburg, Austria.

When he was just three years old, he learned to play the harpsichord.

By the time he was five years old, he was composing music.

At the age of six, he was invited to perform for the Empress of Austria.

Mozart's father, Leopold, was a well-known musician who took Mozart on tours through Europe.

Mozart performed for kings and queens, for other musicians, and in churches.

In 1781, Mozart left his hometown and moved to Vienna, Austria.

He earned a living by selling the music that he wrote, giving music lessons, and performing his music in public.

From "The Music of Mozart" by Stephanie Zurich in *World Facts Encyclopedia, 1999 edition, vol. 10, p: 136–137.*

Mozart's compositions included operas, symphonies, concertos, serenades, and church music.

Mozart wrote 22 operas including *The Marriage of Figaro*, *Don Giovanni*, and *The Magic Flute*.

Today, *Don Giovanni* is considered the world's greatest opera.

Mozart wrote at least 40 symphonies for orchestras.

His most famous work is called *Requiem*. *Requiem* was a mass, or prayers, for the dead.

From the book *Great Composers of Our Time* **by Tyler Brown. Brownberry Publishing 1999.**

Mozart died a poor man on December 5, 1791, at the age of 35.

Today, Mozart is considered to have been a musical genius.

His music is known throughout the world.

GO

Name _____ Date _____

_____

_____

_____

_____

_____

_____

_____

_____

_____

_____

_____

_____

_____

_____

_____

_____

_____

_____

_____

_____

_____

DIRECTIONS: Complete the bibliography using information from the facts on the previous page.

Brown, Tyler _____
                                      (title, publisher, date)

Morrow, _____
               (article, magazine, volume, date, page number

_____
               (author last name, first name, article, encyclopedia, date, volume, page number)

STOP

Interpreting Writing

> **February 9**
>
> Tomorrow is the big day. I've studied so hard for the past three weeks that I think I could spell these words in my sleep. But what if I get nervous and mess up? What if someone else knows more words than I know? Rebecca always wins when we practice at school. I just want to do the best that I can. Mom has helped me every night after supper. She says that studying and learning are more important, in the long run, than winning. I guess she's right. But I still really hope I win.
>
> **February 10**
>
> I did it! Well, I didn't win first place, but I came in second. And I'm really proud of that. At first, I was scared when I looked out and saw all those people in the audience. I was afraid I'd forget everything. But then I told myself, "You studied hard. You know all those words. Come on, you can do it!" My first word was indicate: i-n-d-i-c-a-t-e. It was easy. Then I knew I could do the rest of them, too. The only word that really stumped me was cannibal. I spelled it c-a-n-n-i-b-l-e—oops. Rebecca spelled it right, along with her last word: hydraulics. Oh well, I won a dictionary and had my picture taken for the newspaper. When I came home, my family had a party to celebrate! Tomorrow, I start studying for next year's contest.

DIRECTIONS: Answer the following questions about Ben's journal entries.

1. What big event was Ben writing about in his journal?

Spelling Bee

2. What word best describes how Ben was feeling the day before the event?

- Ⓐ confident
- Ⓑ anxious
- Ⓒ tired
- Ⓓ happy

3. Which phrase best describes how Ben felt about winning second place?

- Ⓕ upset because he didn't win first place
- Ⓖ angry at the person who beat him
- Ⓗ happy because he did his best
- Ⓙ disappointed and ready to give up

4. How did Ben get over his fear of being in front of an audience?

- Ⓐ by practicing in front of a mirror
- Ⓑ by telling himself, "you can do it!"
- Ⓒ by closing his eyes
- Ⓓ by telling himself he didn't care if he won or lost

5. Which sentence best describes how Ben prepared for the contest?

- Ⓕ He looked over the list just once or twice.
- Ⓖ He studied very hard over a three-week period.
- Ⓗ He thought he could depend on being smart and didn't even look at the words.
- Ⓙ He practiced with his sister.

STOP

Writing

| 2.5 |

Writing a Persuasive Composition

DIRECTIONS: Write a persuasive composition by finishing the thought "The world would be a better place without . . ." State your position clearly, and present evidence for your position. Anticipate and address any points on which your readers may disagree.

_____

_____

_____

_____

_____

_____

_____

_____

_____

_____

_____

_____

_____

_____

_____

_____

_____

_____

_____

_____

_____

_____

STOP

Writing

2.0

For pages 57–62

| Mini-Test 2 |

Writing Applications

DIRECTIONS: Katie is writing an essay comparing the architecture used in different places of the world throughout history. Keep this in mind when you do questions 1 and 2.

1. **What would be a good method for Katie to use to organize her essay?**

   Ⓐ compare noted buildings from the same time period but in one place, like Europe

   Ⓑ examine the materials used for historic buildings throughout the United States

   Ⓒ examine the methods people used to move large stones in Egypt, South America, and Asia

   Ⓓ compare noted buildings from the same time period but in different places throughout the world

2. **To begin her report, Katie wants to read general information about architecture and its history. Which of these should she use?**

   Ⓕ a book on world history

   Ⓖ an encyclopedia

   Ⓗ the biography of a famous architect

   Ⓙ a thesaurus

For question 3, choose the notes that Katie might write when she reads the following information.

3. **Builders throughout the world have used the pyramid shape for constructing large buildings and memorials. They have also depended on available materials such as wood from nearby forests or stone from local quarries.**

   Ⓐ most pyramids made of wood or stone

   Ⓑ large buildings and memorials; pyramids made of wood or stone

   Ⓒ builders used pyramid shape; depended on available materials

   Ⓓ builders in many places; pyramids; wood and stone

DIRECTIONS: Find the best topic sentence for each of the paragraphs below.

4. **_____. The inside of the plant is like a sponge that holds water during long dry spells. The outside of the cactus is a waxy skin that prevents water inside the plant from evaporating during hot days. The sharp spines of a cactus prevent animals from eating them.**

   Ⓕ For a short period of time in the spring, a cactus plant has a beautiful flower.

   Ⓖ Some cactus plants in the Arizona desert are hundreds of years old.

   Ⓗ Cactus plants are perfectly adapted to a desert environment.

   Ⓙ Experienced desert travelers know that a cactus plant is an important source of water.

5. **_____. She had painted for more than sixty years, but had shown her work to no one other than her husband. A friend had discovered her paintings accidentally and told Mrs. McClellan she should show them. At the age of seventy-eight, she was having her first art show.**

   Ⓐ Art is often a very private thing.

   Ⓑ It was one of the proudest moments of Mrs. McClellan's life.

   Ⓒ Talent emerges in some people very late in life.

   Ⓓ Mrs. McClellan had always lived what she considered to be a normal life.

How Am I Doing?

Mini-Test 1 Page 55 **Number Correct** ☐	**4** answers correct	**Great Job!** Move on to the section test on page 65.
	3 answers correct	**You're almost there!** But you still need a little practice. Review practice pages 51–54 before moving on to the section test on page 65.
	0–2 answers correct	**Oops!** Time to review what you have learned and try again. Review the practice section on pages 51–54. Then retake the test on page 55. Now move on to the section test on page 65.
Mini-Test 2 Page 63 **Number Correct** ☐	**5** answers correct	**Awesome!** Move on to the section test on page 65.
	3–4 answers correct	**You're almost there!** But you still need a little practice. Review practice pages 57–62 before moving on to the section test on page 65.
	0–2 answers correct	**Oops!** Time to review what you have learned and try again. Review the practice section on pages 57–62. Then retake the test on page 63. Now move on to the section test on page 65.

Name _____   Date _____

Final Writing Test
for pages 50–63

DIRECTIONS: Choose the form of writing that would best suit the author's stated purpose.

1. **The author wants to tell her mother about her new job.**
   - Ⓐ a personal letter
   - Ⓑ a report
   - Ⓒ a business letter
   - Ⓓ a letter to the editor

2. **The author wants to respond to an editorial in yesterday's newspaper.**
   - Ⓕ a personal letter
   - Ⓖ a letter to the editor
   - Ⓗ a report
   - Ⓙ a review

3. **The author wants to share what he learned about the history of NASA.**
   - Ⓐ a poem
   - Ⓑ a letter to the editor
   - Ⓒ a review
   - Ⓓ a report

4. **The author wants to tell his classmates about a great book.**
   - Ⓕ a personal letter
   - Ⓖ a review
   - Ⓗ a poem
   - Ⓙ a letter to the editor

5. **The author wants to sell her bike.**
   - Ⓐ a classified ad
   - Ⓑ an ad in the Yellow Pages
   - Ⓒ a personal letter
   - Ⓓ an editorial

DIRECTIONS: Read the paragraph, then answer the questions.

(1) "This is a pretty good poem," she thought to herself. (2) "It's just that . . . " (3) Lois wondered if she had fed her dog before she left for school. (4) Then her name was called, she stood up, and her knees began to shake. (5) When she turned around and looked at the rest of the class, however, she saw friendly faces.

6. **Choose the best first sentence for this paragraph.**
   - Ⓕ Lois waited for her turn to read her poem in front of the class.
   - Ⓖ Lois could hardly wait to go to lunch.
   - Ⓗ Lois was looking forward to reading her play.
   - Ⓙ Lois loved English class.

7. **Which sentence should be left out of this paragraph?**
   - Ⓐ Sentence 1
   - Ⓑ Sentence 2
   - Ⓒ Sentence 3
   - Ⓓ Sentence 5

8. **Choose the best last sentence for this paragraph.**
   - Ⓕ "Oh, no," she remembered, "I didn't feed the dog."
   - Ⓖ Lois felt like running from the room.
   - Ⓗ Lois decided that this would be a great time to read all of her poems.
   - Ⓙ "Maybe this won't be so bad after all," Lois thought with relief.

DIRECTIONS: Read the passage, then answer the questions.

(1) <u>The weather was bad</u> over the mid-Atlantic Ocean. (2) The small plane's engine sputtered. (3) The slim, young woman at the controls knew she was too far out to turn back. (4) Carefully she coaxed the plane ahead through the storm. (5) When dawn came, the engine was failing seriously. (6) Just ahead lay the Irish coast. (7) As the engine gasped its last breath, the woman brought her plane down in a cow pasture.

(8) An astonished farmer raced over as the young woman climbed out of the airplane. (9) "I'm from America," she said. (10) "My name is Amelia Earhart." (11) The farmer was angry that she had ruined part of his field. (12) She had even set a new speed record: thirteen hours and thirty minutes!

(13) They didn't think a woman was strong enough to keep going through the long night. (14) However, Earhart had strength and courage to spare. (15) She had already made parachute jumps and had explored the ocean floor in a diver's suit. (16) Now, overnight, she had become famous.

9. **Which sentence could replace sentence 11?**

Ⓐ The farmer thought she was an alien.

Ⓑ She had become the first woman to fly over the Atlantic Ocean alone.

Ⓒ She had become the first woman to safely land in a pasture.

Ⓓ She added, "Do you know where I might get something good to eat?"

10. **Which sentence could begin the third paragraph?**

Ⓕ Many people had told Amelia not to make this flight.

Ⓖ Amelia wanted to give up.

Ⓗ Amelia was a weak woman.

Ⓙ Amelia loved to set world records.

11. **Which group of words would be more colorful than the underlined words in sentence 1?**

Ⓐ There was lightning

Ⓑ Lightning ripped through the blackness

Ⓒ It was cold and wet

Ⓓ The weather was stormy

12. **Which sentence does not belong in the story?**

Ⓕ Sentence 2

Ⓖ Sentence 6

Ⓗ Sentence 11

Ⓙ Sentence 16

DIRECTIONS: Read the following passages, then answer the questions.

Act 1 Airport, early morning

Young Ty Waalkes and his best friend Drew Moore prepare to leave home for the International Scholastic Problem Solvers Finale in Singapore. At the airport, Ty learns that his parents' business is on the edge of bankruptcy. Ty's friend Gracie did not come to the airport to say good-bye. They had a fight yesterday. Ty's kid brother, Charlie, gruffly informs him that this morning he lost Ty's pet rat. The family bids a fond farewell to the two travelers. Everyone wishes them well in the tournament.

Act 2 Over the Pacific, early afternoon

Ty and Drew are guided to Concourse G, Gate 54. Here they are informed that the problem-solving simulation will begin momentarily. The boys board what appears to be a Boeing 737, where they are awed by their fellow "passengers." A man across the aisle constantly pecks away at his laptop and yells into his cell phone. A woman three seats ahead has two children in tow. She is returning from the Teenie Tots of the World beauty contest.

GO →

She angrily rants about cheating judges overlooking her precious jewels. Shortly after take off, a peculiarly secretive elderly woman tries to sell the boys unusual items, such as jewelry and electronics. During a meal of ham sandwiches and caviar, the "passengers" are interrupted by a frantic announcement from the pilot. He informs them that birds have been sucked into all four engines and that the plane is losing altitude. Suddenly the plane drops.

Act 3 On a life raft in the Pacific, two days later

The simulation continues as Ty awakens on a raft floating out in open sea. He performs first aid on Drew, who is not feeling well. They share their raft with Blair, one of the child modeling contestants; the strange elderly woman; an airline steward named Hal, who reminds Ty of a giant dinosaur; and a fellow student, Chloe, who is also part of the International Scholastic Problem Solvers Finale. As their raftmates' behaviors become increasingly erratic, the three young people take over. They teach the elderly woman and steward how to catch fish and albatross and how to construct a shelter using blankets, shirts, and rubber bands provided by Blair. Ty teaches his five mates a song to keep their spirits up. Chloe and the recovered Drew restrain the steward from drowning himself in the shark-infested waters. At dusk, just as their water supply runs out, the elderly woman spies land to the southwest.

Act 4 Singapore harbor, night to dawn

Harbor lights appear in the distance. The raftmates enthusiastically paddle their craft to shore. Upon arrival, the three students learn that the elderly woman is actually a judge for the Problem Solvers Finale. By microphone and hidden camera, a team of judges has observed the students from a booth high over the set's ceiling.

The audio and videotapes clearly detail the children's progress. Because of their stellar actions, the three win the contest, and they each receive a full college scholarship to a university of their choice. The contest officials arrange to market Ty's parents' product worldwide, thus saving their business. Drew, Chloe, and Ty are interviewed by all of the major television networks. Within minutes, Ty's friend Gracie tearfully calls, begging forgiveness. Hand in hand, Ty, Chloe, and Drew step from the virtual reality set and greet the setting sun.

13. **What is the setting for Act 1?**
   - (A) the airplane
   - (B) the airport
   - (C) Singapore harbor
   - (D) on a life raft

14. **What is the purpose of this story?**
   - (F) to inform
   - (G) to entertain
   - (H) to expose
   - (J) to illustrate

15. **From what point of view is the story told?**
   - (A) first person
   - (B) second person
   - (C) third person
   - (D) none of these

16. **What can you conclude about the Problem Solvers Finale organization?**
   - (F) they are sneaky
   - (G) they are generous
   - (H) neither of these
   - (J) both of these

GO

17. Which of the following would be most appropriate in a letter asking permission to hold a car wash in a store's parking lot?

(A) Your store is the best grocery store in Orchard Grove. My parents buy all their groceries at your store. Our class is trying to raise money for a class trip. We would like to hold a car wash in your parking lot on Saturday, because we would get lots of business on that day.

(B) We have 25 students in our class. Our teacher's name is Mr. Wordsworth. He is a great teacher. He said I should write to ask if we could hold a car wash in your parking lot on Saturday. He thought you would say yes.

(C) The students in our class are raising money for our class trip. We would like your permission to hold a car wash in your parking lot on Saturday from 9:00 A.M. to 3 P.M. We promise to clean up when we are finished. We appreciate your consideration of this matter.

(D) The students in our class think the best place to have a car wash would be in your parking lot. We think we could raise lots of money there. We need money to go on a class trip, since the school will not pay our way. Saturday from 9:00 A.M. to 3 P.M. would be a great time for us.

DIRECTIONS: Choose the correct form for each bibliography entry.

18. a book called *Everyday Life on the Prairie*, written by Marsha Yolen. Published by Standard Publishing in 1984

(F) *Everyday Life on the Prairie*, Yolen, Marsha. Standard Publishing, 1984

(G) Marsha Yolen's *Everyday Life on the Prairie*,1984.

(H) Yolen, Marsha, *Everyday Life on the Prairie*, Standard Publishing, 1984.

(J) *Everyday Life on the Prairie* by Marsha Yolen, Standard, 1984.

19. a magazine article called "Life as a Settler," written by Paul Barker. It appeared on pages 54–57 of volume 31 of the magazine *World History* published in July of 1995

(A) Barker, Paul, "Life as a Settler," *World History*, (vol. 31), July 1995, pp. 54–57.

(B) *World History*, (vol. 31), July 1995, pp. 54–57, "Life as a Settler," by Paul Barker

(C) "Life as a Settler," by Paul Barker. *World History*, July 1995, pp. 54–57

(D) Barker, Paul. "Life as a Settler," *World History*, (vol. 31), July 1995.

Name _____ Date _____

Final Writing Test
Answer Sheet

1 Ⓐ Ⓑ Ⓒ Ⓓ
2 Ⓕ Ⓖ Ⓗ Ⓙ
3 Ⓐ Ⓑ Ⓒ Ⓓ
4 Ⓕ Ⓖ Ⓗ Ⓙ
5 Ⓐ Ⓑ Ⓒ Ⓓ
6 Ⓕ Ⓖ Ⓗ Ⓙ
7 Ⓐ Ⓑ Ⓒ Ⓓ
8 Ⓕ Ⓖ Ⓗ Ⓙ
9 Ⓐ Ⓑ Ⓒ Ⓓ
10 Ⓕ Ⓖ Ⓗ Ⓙ

11 Ⓐ Ⓑ Ⓒ Ⓓ
12 Ⓕ Ⓖ Ⓗ Ⓙ
13 Ⓐ Ⓑ Ⓒ Ⓓ
14 Ⓕ Ⓖ Ⓗ Ⓙ
15 Ⓐ Ⓑ Ⓒ Ⓓ
16 Ⓕ Ⓖ Ⓗ Ⓙ
17 Ⓐ Ⓑ Ⓒ Ⓓ
18 Ⓕ Ⓖ Ⓗ Ⓙ
19 Ⓐ Ⓑ Ⓒ Ⓓ

Written and Oral English Language Convention Standards

The standards for written and oral English language conventions have been placed between those for writing and for listening and speaking because these conventions are essential to both sets of skills.

1.0 Written and Oral English Language Conventions
Students write and speak with a command of standard English conventions appropriate to this grade level.

Sentence Structure
1.1 Use simple, compound, and compound-complex sentences; use effective coordination and subordination of ideas to express complete thoughts. *(See page 72.)*

What it means:
- coordination of ideas: combining sentences that have two equally important ideas by using conjunctions such as and, or, neither . . . nor, not only . . . but also, and so forth. Example: I need to give the dog a bath and clean my bedroom.
- subordination of ideas: combining sentences that have ideas that are not equally important by using subordinating conjunctions such as although, because, or unless; the idea that is less important becomes a subordinate clause. Example: Although I arrived on time, the show didn't start until nine.

Grammar
1.2 Identify and properly use indefinite pronouns and present perfect, past perfect, and future perfect verb tenses; ensure that verbs agree with compound subjects. *(See page 73.)*

What it means:
- indefinite pronouns: pronouns that generally refer to people, places, things, or ideas. Example: another, many, someone
- present perfect: verb tense that expresses an action or condition that occurred at an indefinite time in the past; formed by combining has or have with the past participle of a verb. Example: has begun, have built
- past perfect: verb tense that is used to convey that one action began and ended before another action started; formed by using the auxiliary verb had with the past participle of a verb. Example: had begun, had built
- future perfect: verb tense that implies that one future action will begin and end before another future action begins; formed by combining will have or shall have with the past participle of a verb. Example: will have begun, will have built

Punctuation
1.3 Use colons after the salutation in business letters, semicolons to connect independent clauses, and commas when linking two clauses with a conjunction in compound sentences. *(See page 74.)*

Capitalization
1.4 Use correct capitalization. *(See page 75.)*

Spelling
1.5 Spell frequently misspelled words correctly (e.g., their, they're, there). *(See page 76.)*

Listening and Speaking Standards

NOTE: The California content standards for Listening and Speaking skills are listed here so that you can practice them on your own with your student.

1.0 Listening and Speaking Strategies
Students deliver focused, coherent presentations that convey ideas clearly and relate to the background and interests of the audience. They evaluate the content of oral communication.

Comprehension

1.1 Relate the speaker's verbal communication (e.g., word choice, pitch, feeling, tone) to the nonverbal message (e.g., posture, gesture).

1.2 Identify the tone, mood, and emotion conveyed in the oral communication.

1.3 Restate and execute multiple-step oral instructions and directions.

Organization and Delivery of Oral Communication

1.4 Select a focus, an organizational structure, and a point of view, matching the purpose, message, occasion, and vocal modulation to the audience.

1.5 Emphasize salient points to assist the listener in following the main ideas and concepts.

1.6 Support opinions with detailed evidence and with visual or media displays that use appropriate technology.

1.7 Use effective rate, volume, pitch, and tone and align nonverbal elements to sustain audience interest and attention.

Analysis and Evaluation of Oral and Media Communications

1.8 Analyze the use of rhetorical devices (e.g., cadence, repetitive patterns, use of onomatopoeia) for intent and effect.

1.9 Identify persuasive and propaganda techniques used in television and identify false and misleading information.

2.0 Speaking Applications (Genres and Their Characteristics)
Students deliver well-organized formal presentations employing traditional rhetorical strategies (e.g., narration, exposition, persuasion, description). Using the speaking strategies of grade six outlined in Listening and Speaking Standard 1.0, students:

2.1 Deliver narrative presentations:
   a. Establish a context, plot, and point of view.
   b. Include sensory details and concrete language to develop the plot and character.
   c. Use a range of narrative devices (e.g., dialogue, tension, or suspense).

2.2 Deliver informative presentations:
   a. Pose relevant questions sufficiently limited in scope to be completely and thoroughly answered.
   b. Develop the topic with facts, details, examples, and explanations from multiple authoritative sources (e.g., speakers, periodicals, online information).

2.3 Deliver oral responses to literature:
   a. Develop an interpretation exhibiting careful reading, understanding, and insight.
   b. Organize the selected interpretation around several clear ideas, premises, or images.
   c. Develop and justify the selected interpretation through sustained use of examples and textual evidence.

2.4 Deliver persuasive presentations:
   a. Provide a clear statement of the position.
   b. Include relevant evidence.
   c. Offer a logical sequence of information.
   d. Engage the listener and foster acceptance of the proposition or proposal.

2.5 Deliver presentations on problems and solutions:
   a. Theorize on the causes and effects of each problem and establish connections between the defined problem and at least one solution.
   b. Offer persuasive evidence to validate the definition of the problem and the proposed solutions.

Language Conventions

1.1

Sentence Structure

DIRECTIONS: Write *Simple* on the lines after the simple sentences and *Compound* on the lines after the compound sentences.

1. **It was a beautiful day, and I was ready for adventure.**

   _____

2. **I saw my friend Marcy and invited her to come with me.**

   _____

3. **She strapped on her skates, and she joined me.**

   _____

4. **Marcy and I enjoyed our trip to the park.**

   _____

5. **We reached the park and took a rest.**

   _____

6. **Marcy is new to skating, but I'm not.**

   _____

DIRECTIONS: Choose the answer that best combines the sentences.

7. **Gordon is going to the store.
   Samantha is going with him.**

   Ⓐ Gordon is going to the store and so is Samantha.

   Ⓑ Gordon and Samantha are going to the store.

   Ⓒ To the store, Gordon and Samantha are going.

   Ⓓ Gordon and Samantha to the store are going.

8. **Please go to the refrigerator.
   I would like you to get a soda for me.**

   Ⓕ Please go to the refrigerator to get me a soda.

   Ⓖ Please go to the refrigerator to get me a soda, because I want one.

   Ⓗ For me, please go to the refrigerator to get a soda.

   Ⓙ I would like for you to please go to the refrigerator to get a soda for me.

9. **Ms. Lightfoot loves dancing.
   She goes to the dance studio every day.
   She goes at eight o'clock.**

   Ⓐ Ms. Lightfoot loves dancing, and she goes to the dance studio every day at eight o'clock.

   Ⓑ Ms. Lightfoot goes to the dance studio every day at eight o'clock, because she loves dancing.

   Ⓒ Ms. Lightfoot loves dancing every day at the studio at eight o'clock.

   Ⓓ Every day, Ms. Lightfoot loves going to the dance studio to dance at eight o'clock.

72

Name _____ Date _____

Grammar

Clue The present perfect tense is formed by using the present tense of the helping verb *to have* plus the past tense of the verb it helps. The future perfect tense is formed by using the future tense of the helping verb *to have* plus the future tense of the verb it helps.

DIRECTIONS: Use *have, has, had,* or *will have* to complete each sentence.

1. More _____ arrived since the first shipment was sent.

2. Several _____ gone to the wrong address and were returned.

3. Everyone _____ been employed for 5 years by September.

4. Nothing _____ been done to correct the situation until recently.

5. Nobody _____ ventured out since the weather had turned cooler.

6. Many _____ tried to crack the mysterious code, but none have succeeded.

7. No one _____ worked as hard as Igor this month.

8. Somebody _____ been using my chair while I've been gone.

9. Neither _____ taken the opportunity presented to them in the past.

10. All _____ received some training by the end of the term.

11. Each _____ one vote in the upcoming election.

12. Both _____ finished their homework by the time Dad gets home.

13. Most _____ eaten dinner before they left home that night.

14. Few _____ taken the kinds of chances Derek did.

15. Some _____ forgotten to bring their uniforms today.

DIRECTIONS: Circle the correct word to complete each sentence.

16. Both Sam and Caleb **seem/seems** to enjoy their classes.

17. Either Michelle or Rory **want/wants** to be class president.

18. Neither the dog nor the cat **like/likes** the new food.

19. The fern and the lily **need/needs** to be repotted.

20. Richard and I **enjoy/enjoys** planning parties.

21. The Browns and the Hoods **is/are** on vacation this week.

22. Neither the computer nor the printer **work/works** since the storm.

Language Conventions
1.3

Written and Oral English
Language Conventions

Punctuation

Clue   Remember that commas separate clauses. Semicolons can replace conjunctions and connect two related independent clauses.

DIRECTIONS: Correctly place commas or semicolons in the sentences below.

1. Marcy and I bolted from the car and we raced to the duck pond.

2. At first, Marcy was ahead I was behind by only a second.

3. Then Marcy speeded up and I got out of breath.

4. Soon Marcy passed me I didn't have a chance.

5. Marcy was really flying but she didn't look where she was going.

6. The duck pond was right in front of Marcy but she couldn't stop.

7. Marcy had to stop or she would land right in the duck pond.

8. Suddenly, there was a splash all the ducks were squawking.

9. A large, featherless object had just landed in their little world and they were not happy.

10. Marcy had made a big splash but she had won the race.

DIRECTIONS: Write each of the following using the correct punctuation.

11. Closing:
    sincerely

    _____

12. Greeting of a business letter:
    dear sir

    _____

13. Write a greeting to a friend.

    _____

14. Greeting of a business letter:
    dear ms. sorenson

    _____

15. Greeting of a friendly letter:
    dear Julie

    _____

16. Write a greeting to your mom.

    _____

STOP

Language Conventions

1.4

Capitalization

DIRECTIONS: Rewrite the following sentences using the correct capitalization.

1. The proclamation of 1763 forbade British subjects to settle beyond the appalachian mountains.

   _____

   _____

   _____

2. During the revolutionary war, fighting occurred from quebec in the north to florida in the south.

   _____

   _____

   _____

3. The Americans were angry about paying the taxes required by the stamp act of 1765.

   _____

   _____

   _____

4. The boston tea party was planned to protest the tea act of 1773.

   _____

   _____

5. In 1853, the gadsden purchase gave our country more land.

   _____

   _____

6. The mississippi river divides illinois and missouri.

   _____

7. The mojave desert is south of the sierra nevada mountains.

   _____

   _____

8. Pikes peak is in the rocky mountains.

   _____

   _____

9. Cleveland, ohio, is on the border of lake erie.

   _____

   _____

10. California, oregon, and washington are bordered by the pacific ocean.

    _____

    _____

    _____

11. The battle of bull run was one of the first major battles of the civil war.

    _____

    _____

    _____

12. Abraham lincoln gave a famous speech after the battle of gettysburg.

    _____

    _____

    _____

Language Conventions

1.5

Spelling

DIRECTIONS: Fill in the blank with the word that best fits each sentence.

1. **No one wanted to _____ the book with the wrinkled cover.**

   by, buy

2. **The cost of the newspaper has increased to seventy-five _____.**

   cents, sense

3. **Jamal, the social studies report is _____ tomorrow!**

   do, dew, due

4. **Call me when _____ my turn to use the computer.**

   it's, its

5. **We can rest when _____ is nothing left to put away.**

   their, there, they're

6. **The keys were _____ on the table this morning.**

   here, hear

7. **We'll get tickets when _____ in town next year.**

   their, there, they're

8. **Nathan _____ a chapter of the book every day after dinner.**

   red, read

9. **Aunt Jess _____ the package to me on Monday.**

   sent, cent, scent

10. **The car is parked in _____ usual space.**

    it's, its

11. **Chad and Greg brought _____ younger brother to the meeting.**

    their, there, they're

12. **Turner watched the catcher's sign, then _____ a perfect curve ball.**

    threw, through

13. **Nikki _____ the class in singing the national anthem.**

    led, lead

14. **Show Brendan _____ we keep the extra towels**

    where, wear

15. **Put _____ backpack on the shelf by the door.**

    your, you're

16. **_____ going to be here any minute!**

    Their, There, They're

17. **I can't believe _____ time to go already.**

    it's, its

18. **Remember, _____ responsible for returning the videos.**

    your, you're

STOP

Language Conventions

1.0

For pages 72–76

Mini-Test 1

DIRECTIONS: Choose the answer that shows the best capitalization and punctuation.

1. **His family is from Austin, the capital of the state of Texas.**
   - (A) Austin. the
   - (B) Austin. The
   - (C) Austin the
   - (D) Correct as it is

2. **Jennifer loves fish; Tess loathes it.**
   - (F) fish, Tess
   - (G) fish: Tess
   - (H) fish. Tess
   - (J) Correct as it is

3. **Grandma will sit next to me, and, Grandpa will sit by you.**
   - (A) me And
   - (B) me and,
   - (C) me, and
   - (D) Correct as it is

4. **Yoshi spent a week at a sports camp, next year he hopes to go for two weeks.**
   - (F) camp: next
   - (G) camp. Next
   - (H) camp. next
   - (J) Correct as it is

5. **Dear sir: I am writing to request a brochure of the Autumn Memories vacation cottage.**
   - (A) Dear Sir, I am writing
   - (B) Dear Sir: I am writing
   - (C) Dear sir, I am writing
   - (D) Correct as it is

DIRECTIONS: Circle the correct word to complete the following sentences.

6. **They're/Their** planning to be here by noon tomorrow.

7. Everything should be in **it's/its** correct place when you are finished.

8. **Your/You're** cousins will be so excited to see you.

9. Most of the guests **will have/had** gone by the time we arrived.

10. Somebody **has/have** chosen the red and white streamers.

DIRECTIONS: Rewrite the following sentences using the correct capitalization.

11. **Florida is bordered by the gulf of mexico on the west and the atlantic ocean on the east.**

   _____

   _____

   _____

12. **The missouri and mississippi rivers meet at st. louis, missouri.**

   _____

   _____

13. **North carolina, south carolina, and georgia are bordered by the atlantic ocean.**

   _____

   _____

STOP

How Am I Doing?

Mini-Test 1 Page 77 **Number Correct**	**11–13** answers correct	**Great Job!** Move on to the section test on page 79.
	6–10 answers correct	**You're almost there!** But you still need a little practice. Review practice pages 72–76 before moving on to the section test on page 79.
	0–5 answers correct	**Oops!** Time to review what you have learned and try again. Review the practice section on pages 72–76. Then retake the test on page 77. Now move on to the section test on page 79.

Final Language Conventions Test
for pages 72–77

DIRECTIONS: Read the passage below, then answer the questions.

(1) Last May our centennial anniversary for our town was celebrated by us. (2) We made a lot of preparations. (3) A cleanup committee washed all public buildings. (4) They also swept all public buildings. (5) Members of the fire department climbed on high ladders to hang up flags and bunting. (6) At last the celebration began. (7) The high point was when Mayor Lopez asked Olga Janssen—at 105, our oldest citizen—what she remembered about the old days. (8) Mrs. Janssen recalled how her mother had used a churn to make butter, and her favorite memory was of playing dominoes with her cousins. (9) At the end, we all drank a ginger ale toast to the town's next century. (10) We knew most of us would not be here for the next celebration, but we felt happy to be at this one. (11) A large bell was struck with a mallet by the mayor to officially close our celebration.

1. How is sentence 1 best written?

(A) Last May our town's centennial anniversary was celebrated by us.

(B) Last May, we celebrated our town's centennial anniversary.

(C) We celebrated last May our town's centennial anniversary.

(D) As it is

2. How are sentences 3 and 4 best combined?

(F) A cleanup committee washed all public buildings and then swept them.

(G) A cleanup committee washed, and they also swept, all public buildings.

(H) A cleanup committee washed and swept all public buildings.

(J) As it is

3. Sentence 11 is best written—

(A) The mayor officially closed our celebration with a mallet by striking a large bell.

(B) Striking a large bell with a mallet, our celebration officially closed by the mayor.

(C) To officially close our celebration, the mayor struck a large bell with a rubber mallet.

(D) As it is

4. Which sentence should be broken into two sentences?

(F) 2

(G) 5

(H) 8

(J) 10

DIRECTIONS: Choose the best answer.

5. I have _____ people from many countries.

(A) knew

(B) known

(C) knowed

(D) knewn

6. He _____ from the bully who picked on him.

(F) running

(G) run

(H) ran

(J) runned

GO

7. We often have _____ that hard work will get you ahead.

   (A) said

   (B) says

   (C) sayed

   (D) say

8. If you have _____ me a present, I hope it's something I don't have.

   (F) bringed

   (G) broughten

   (H) brought

   (J) bringing

9. After he _____ the ball, he made a home run.

   (A) hitted

   (B) hit

   (C) hitten

   (D) hat

10. After he _____ of the idea, he _____ us about it.

   (F) thinked, told

   (G) thought, telled

   (H) thought, told

   (J) thinks, told

11. She _____ him come in from the rain with wet boots.

   (A) letted

   (B) let

   (C) letten

   (D) lot

12. They have _____ that movie every day this week.

   (F) saw

   (G) seen

   (H) seed

   (J) sawn

13. If you have _____ for the money I owe you, it's right here.

   (A) come

   (B) came

   (C) camed

   (D) comen

14. When we _____ to the store, there was a big sale.

   (F) went

   (G) goed

   (H) wented

   (J) going

DIRECTIONS: Read the passage, then answer the questions.

(1) For many years, people in the United States used streetcars to travel in cities. (2) At first, streetcars were called *horse cars* because horses pulled them. (3) Later, streetcars were powered by steam in the 1800s, people tried to use electric power, but making electricity was considered to be too expensive. (4) In 1888, a machine was invented that made electricity inexpensively. (5) In that same year, the first electric powered streetcars were put into use they quickly replaced the steam-powered streetcar. (6) With the invention of the gas engine electric streetcars were soon replaced by buses and cars. (7) By 1930, the streetcar had begun to disappear from city streets. (8) Interest in streetcars revived in the 1970s.

15. In sentence 2, _horse cars_ **because** is best written —

   (A) horse cars; because

   (B) horse cars, because

   (C) horse cars. Because

   (D) As it is

GO

16. In sentence 3, <u>steam in</u> is best written —

   (F) steam; in

   (G) steam, in

   (H) steam. In

   (J) As it is

17. In sentence 5, <u>use they</u> is best written —

   (A) use: They

   (B) use because they

   (C) use; they

   (D) As it is

18. In sentence 6, <u>gas engine electric</u> is best written —

   (F) gas, engine, electric

   (G) gas, engine electric

   (H) gas engine, electric

   (J) As it is

DIRECTIONS: Choose the sentence that uses correct capitalization.

19. (A) My Friend Jim likes to explore our city

     (B) My friend jim likes to explore our city.

     (C) My friend Jim likes to explore our city.

     (D) My friend Jim likes to explore our City.

20. (F) Last week, Jim visited the Natural History Museum.

     (G) Last week, jim visited the natural history museum.

     (H) Last week, Jim visited the natural history museum.

     (J) Last week, Jim visited the Natural History museum.

21. (A) His Uncle Jasper took him to see the Dallas museum of art.

     (B) His uncle Jasper took him to see the Dallas Museum of Art.

     (C) His Uncle Jasper took him to see the dallas Museum of Art.

     (D) His uncle Jasper took him to see the Dallas museum of art.

22. (F) Jim enjoyed seeing the paintings at the museum.

     (G) Jim enjoyed seeing the paintings at the Museum.

     (H) Jim enjoyed seeing the Paintings at the Museum.

     (J) Jim enjoyed seeing the Paintings at the museum.

23. (A) Next, jim wants to go to the Texas State Fair.

     (B) Next, Jim wants to go to the Texas State Fair.

     (C) Next, Jim wants to go to the Texas state fair.

     (D) Next, Jim wants to go to the Texas State fair.

24. (F) The fair is held at fair park every October.

     (G) The fair is held at Fair park every October.

     (H) The fair is held at Fair Park every October.

     (J) The fair is held at Fair Park every october.

Name _____ Date _____

25. **(1)** It's too bad that dogs can't talk.
    (2) That dog would bite it's master if it had the chance.
    (3) You just don't know their dog, Wally.
    (4) I saw him over their waiting for trouble.

    Ⓐ 1 and 2
    Ⓑ 3 and 4
    Ⓒ 1 and 3
    Ⓓ 2 and 3

26. **(5)** Well, they're crazy about their dog.
    (6) If he was you're dog, you'd feel differently.
    (7) He's licking you're face!
    (8) It's true; he's a nice dog!

    Ⓕ 6 and 7
    Ⓖ 5 and 8
    Ⓗ 7 and 8
    Ⓙ 5 and 7

27. **We have a television in our family room. We enjoy watching television together as a family.**

    Ⓐ In the family room is our television, which we enjoy together as a family.
    Ⓑ Our television is in the family room, which my family enjoys together.
    Ⓒ My family enjoys watching television together in the family room.
    Ⓓ My family enjoys in the family room watching television.

28. **There was a very heavy rain. The police officer said we would have to take a detour.**

    Ⓕ Because of the heavy rain, we had to take a detour the police officer said.
    Ⓖ The police officer said because of the heavy rain, we had to take a detour.
    Ⓗ The police officer said we would have to take a detour because of the heavy rain.
    Ⓙ We had to take a detour, said the police officer, in spite of the heavy rain.

Name _____ Date _____

Final Language Conventions Test
Answer Sheet

1 (A) (B) (C) (D)
2 (F) (G) (H) (J)
3 (A) (B) (C) (D)
4 (F) (G) (H) (J)
5 (A) (B) (C) (D)
6 (F) (G) (H) (J)
7 (A) (B) (C) (D)
8 (F) (G) (H) (J)
9 (A) (B) (C) (D)
10 (F) (G) (H) (J)

11 (A) (B) (C) (D)
12 (F) (G) (H) (J)
13 (A) (B) (C) (D)
14 (F) (G) (H) (J)
15 (A) (B) (C) (D)
16 (F) (G) (H) (J)
17 (A) (B) (C) (D)
18 (F) (G) (H) (J)
19 (A) (B) (C) (D)
20 (F) (G) (H) (J)

21 (A) (B) (C) (D)
22 (F) (G) (H) (J)
23 (A) (B) (C) (D)
24 (F) (G) (H) (J)
25 (A) (B) (C) (D)
26 (F) (G) (H) (J)
27 (A) (B) (C) (D)
28 (F) (G) (H) (J)

California Mathematics
Content Standards

The mathematics content standards developed by the California State Board of Education are divided into five major sections. The information within those sections tell specifically what your sixth-grader should know or be able to do.

1) Number Sense

2) Algebra and Functions

3) Measurement and Geometry

4) Statistics, Data Analysis, and Probability

5) Mathematical Reasoning

Mathematics
Table of Contents

Number Sense Standards

Grade 6 Mathematics Content Standards

By the end of grade six, students have mastered the four arithmetic operations with whole numbers, positive fractions, positive decimals, and positive and negative integers; they accurately compute and solve problems. They apply their knowledge to statistics and probability. Students understand the concepts of mean, median, and mode of data sets and how to calculate the range. They analyze data and sampling processes for possible bias and misleading conclusions; they use addition and multiplication of fractions routinely to calculate the probabilities for compound events. Students conceptually understand and work with ratios and proportions; they compute percentages (e.g., tax, tips, interest). Students know about p and the formulas for the circumference and area of a circle. They use letters for numbers in formulas involving geometric shapes and in ratios to represent an unknown part of an expression. They solve one-step linear equations.

1.0 Students compare and order positive and negative fractions, decimals, and mixed numbers. Students solve problems involving fractions, ratios, proportions, and percentages:

1.1 Compare and order positive and negative fractions, decimals, and mixed numbers and place them on a number line. *(See page 86.)*

1.2 Interpret and use ratios in different contexts (e.g., batting averages, miles per hour) to show the relative sizes of two quantities, using appropriate notations (a/b, a to b, a:b). *(See page 87.)*

1.3 Use proportions to solve problems (e.g., determine the value of N if $\frac{4}{7} = \frac{N}{21}$, find the length of a side of a polygon similar to a known polygon). Use cross-multiplication as a method for solving such problems, understanding it as the multiplication of both sides of an equation by a multiplicative inverse. *(See page 88.)*

What it means:
- Multiplying a number and its inverse results in a product of one. The multiplicative inverse of $\frac{2}{3}$ is $\frac{3}{2}$.

1.4 Calculate given percentages of quantities and solve problems involving discounts at sales, interest earned, and tips. *(See page 89.)*

Math

1.1

Number Sense

Comparing Numbers

Clue Look for key words and numbers that will help you find the answers. Remember, you might not have to compute to find the correct answer to a problem. If a problem is too difficult, skip it and come back to it later.

DIRECTIONS: Use the number line for questions 1–3.

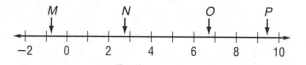

1. On the number line, which arrow points most closely to 2.8?

   (A) M

   (B) N

   (C) O

   (D) P

2. On the number line, which arrow points most closely to $6\frac{3}{4}$?

   (F) M

   (G) N

   (H) O

   (J) P

3. On the number line, which arrow points most closely to −0.8?

   (A) M

   (B) N

   (C) O

   (D) P

4. Which of these values is between 0.07 and 0.5 in value?

   (F) 0.18

   (G) 0.81

   (H) 0.007

   (J) 0.018

5. Which group of decimals is ordered from greatest to least?

   (A) 3.021, 4.123, 0.788, 1.234

   (B) 0.567, 0.870, 0.912, 1.087

   (C) 2.067, 1.989, 1.320, 0.879

   (D) 0.003, 1.076, 0.873, 0.002

6. How many of the fractions listed are greater than $\frac{3}{5}$?

   $$\frac{2}{5}, \frac{3}{4}, \frac{6}{7}, \frac{1}{2}, \frac{20}{25}, \frac{7}{10}$$

   (F) 1

   (G) 3

   (H) 4

   (J) 2

7. Which of these is between 0.08 and 0.4 in value?

   (A) 0.19

   (B) 0.91

   (C) 0.009

   (D) 0.019

8. Which group of decimals is ordered from least to greatest?

   (F) 4.081, 1.804, 10.48, 1.408

   (G) 1.048, 1.408, 1.804, 4.081

   (H) 0.481, 1.408, 4.801, 0.841

   (J) 0.841, 0.481, 8.401, 8.014

Math
1.2

Ratios

DIRECTIONS: Use the table for the example and questions 1–4.

Animal	Number of Students
Sea Lion	6 students
Penguin	14 students
Turtle	11 students
Hammerhead Shark	9 students

1. Which of the following is not the ratio of students who saw sea lions to those who saw turtles?

   (A) $\frac{6}{11}$

   (B) 6 to 11

   (C) 6 – 11

   (D) 6:11

2. What is the ratio of students who saw sea lions to those who saw penguins?

   (F) 14:6

   (G) 6 to 20

   (H) 14:20

   (J) $\frac{6}{14}$

3. What is the ratio of students who saw turtles to those who saw penguins?

   (A) 14 to 11

   (B) $\frac{11}{14}$

   (C) 11 to 25

   (D) 14:25

4. What is the ratio of students who saw hammerhead sharks to those who saw penguins?

   (F) 9:14

   (G) 9:43

   (H) 14:9

   (J) 1:2

DIRECTIONS: For questions 5–7, suppose you had 5 apples, 8 oranges, and 2 bananas.

5. What fraction of the fruit would the apples be?

   (A) $\frac{5}{10}$

   (B) $\frac{1}{5}$

   (C) $\frac{1}{15}$

   (D) $\frac{1}{3}$

6. What fraction of the fruit would the oranges be?

   (F) $\frac{8}{7}$

   (G) $\frac{8}{15}$

   (H) $\frac{1}{2}$

   (J) $\frac{8}{5}$

7. What is the ratio of apples to bananas?

   (A) 5:2

   (B) $\frac{5}{7}$

   (C) 5 to 8

   (D) $\frac{1}{3}$

STOP

Name _____   Date _____

Math

1.3

Proportions

DIRECTIONS: Choose the best answer.

1. $\dfrac{3}{\blacksquare} = \dfrac{18}{36}$

  Ⓐ 5
  Ⓑ 6
  Ⓒ 8
  Ⓓ 4

2. $\dfrac{5}{n} = \dfrac{20}{36}$ $\quad 180 = n20$

  Ⓕ $n = 36$
  Ⓖ $n = 7$
  Ⓗ $n = 9$
  Ⓙ $n = 4$

3. $\dfrac{4}{\blacksquare} = \dfrac{24}{42}$

  Ⓐ 7
  Ⓑ 20
  Ⓒ 14
  Ⓓ 6

4. **Which of these numbers can go in the square to make this number sentence true?**

  $$\dfrac{1}{\blacksquare} > \dfrac{1}{3}$$

  Ⓕ 2
  Ⓖ 3
  Ⓗ 6
  Ⓙ 5

5. **Two triangles are similar. On one triangle, the sides are 4, 5, and 6 units long. The second triangle has sides 8, 10, and x. Use proportions to find x.**

  Ⓐ 14
  Ⓑ 6
  Ⓒ 12
  Ⓓ 10

6. **Find n.** $\dfrac{1}{8} = \dfrac{n}{16}$

  Ⓕ 4
  Ⓖ 8
  Ⓗ 2
  Ⓙ 6

7. **Find n.** $\dfrac{3}{5} = \dfrac{6}{n}$

  Ⓐ 10
  Ⓑ 6
  Ⓒ 3
  Ⓓ 30

8. **Find n.** $\dfrac{12}{n} = \dfrac{1}{3}$

  Ⓕ 6
  Ⓖ 4
  Ⓗ 13
  Ⓙ 36

9. **Find n.** $\dfrac{n}{27} = \dfrac{6}{18}$

  Ⓐ 15
  Ⓑ 3
  Ⓒ 9
  Ⓓ 12

10. **Find n.** $\dfrac{10}{n} = \dfrac{2}{5}$

  Ⓕ 15
  Ⓖ 30
  Ⓗ 25
  Ⓙ 20

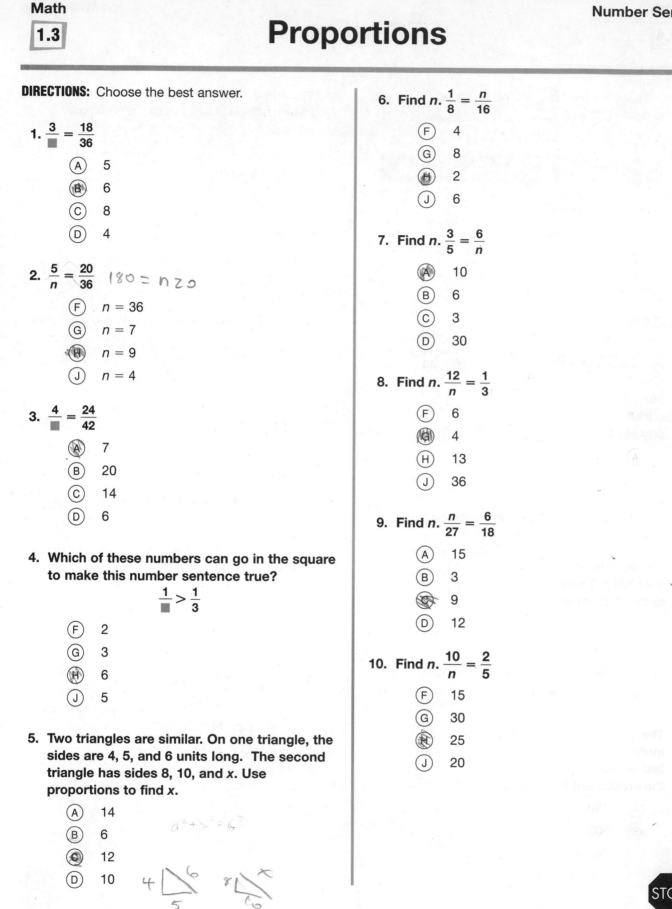

STOP

88

Math
1.4

Percentages

Example:

The enrollment at King School has increased 20% from last year. The enrollment last year was 650. By how many students has the enrollment increased?

- (A) 120
- (B) 130
- (C) 150
- (D) 90

Answer: (B)

DIRECTIONS: Choose the best answer.

1. Pizzazz Pizza Parlor gave the sixth grade class a 25% discount on pizzas they purchased for a party. Each pizza originally cost $12.00. How much did the sixth graders pay per pizza?
   - (A) $3.00
   - (B) $9.00
   - (C) $8.00
   - (D) $6.00

2. Twenty-five percent of the workers are on third shift. There are 132 workers in all. How many of them are on third shift?
   - (F) 25
   - (G) 12
   - (H) 33
   - (J) 3

3. The enrollment at Franklin School has increased 20% from last year. The enrollment last year was 750. By how many students has the enrollment increased?
   - (A) 750
   - (B) 900
   - (C) 600
   - (D) 150

4. Forty percent of the class finished their assignment before lunch. There are 25 students in the class. How many students finished before lunch?
   - (F) 40
   - (G) 10
   - (H) 25
   - (J) 12

5. The tax on a certain item is 10% of the sales price. What would be the amount of tax on an item that sells for $60?
   - (A) $6
   - (B) $10
   - (C) $60
   - (D) $5

6. It is estimated that a new truck will be worth 75% of its original cost after one year. How much would a 1-year-old truck be worth that originally sold for $5,600?
   - (F) $5,600
   - (G) $1,400
   - (H) $4,200
   - (J) $4,000

Math

1.0

For pages 86–89

Mini-Test 1

Number Sense

DIRECTIONS: Choose the best answer. Use the number line for questions 1–3.

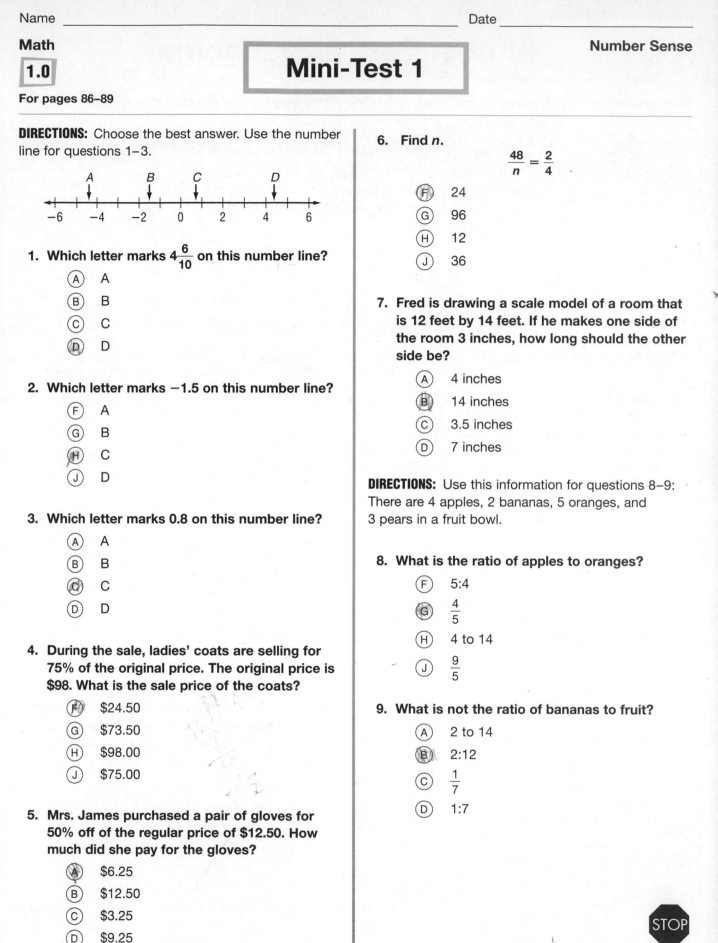

1. Which letter marks $4\frac{6}{10}$ on this number line?

   (A) A

   (B) B

   (C) C

   (D) D

2. Which letter marks −1.5 on this number line?

   (F) A

   (G) B

   (H) C

   (J) D

3. Which letter marks 0.8 on this number line?

   (A) A

   (B) B

   (C) C

   (D) D

4. During the sale, ladies' coats are selling for 75% of the original price. The original price is $98. What is the sale price of the coats?

   (F) $24.50

   (G) $73.50

   (H) $98.00

   (J) $75.00

5. Mrs. James purchased a pair of gloves for 50% off of the regular price of $12.50. How much did she pay for the gloves?

   (A) $6.25

   (B) $12.50

   (C) $3.25

   (D) $9.25

6. Find n.

   $$\frac{48}{n} = \frac{2}{4}$$

   (F) 24

   (G) 96

   (H) 12

   (J) 36

7. Fred is drawing a scale model of a room that is 12 feet by 14 feet. If he makes one side of the room 3 inches, how long should the other side be?

   (A) 4 inches

   (B) 14 inches

   (C) 3.5 inches

   (D) 7 inches

DIRECTIONS: Use this information for questions 8–9: There are 4 apples, 2 bananas, 5 oranges, and 3 pears in a fruit bowl.

8. What is the ratio of apples to oranges?

   (F) 5:4

   (G) $\frac{4}{5}$

   (H) 4 to 14

   (J) $\frac{9}{5}$

9. What is not the ratio of bananas to fruit?

   (A) 2 to 14

   (B) 2:12

   (C) $\frac{1}{7}$

   (D) 1:7

STOP

Number Sense Standards

2.0 Students calculate and solve problems involving addition, subtraction, multiplication, and division:

2.1 Solve problems involving addition, subtraction, multiplication, and division of positive fractions and explain why a particular operation was used for a given situation. *(See page 92.)*

2.2 Explain the meaning of multiplication and division of positive fractions and perform the calculations (e.g., $\frac{5}{8} \div \frac{15}{16} = \frac{5}{8} \times \frac{16}{15} = \frac{2}{3}$). *(See page 93.)*

2.3 Solve addition, subtraction, multiplication, and division problems, including those arising in concrete situations, that use positive and negative integers and combinations of these operations. *(See page 94.)*

2.4 Determine the least common multiple and the greatest common divisor of whole numbers; use them to solve problems with fractions (e.g., to find a common denominator to add two fractions or to find the reduced form for a fraction). *(See page 95.)*

Name _____   Date _____

Solving Problems

DIRECTIONS: Choose the best answer.

1. Matthew spent $\frac{1}{2}$ hour doing his history homework and $\frac{3}{4}$ hour doing his science homework. How many hours did he spend doing his homework?

   (A) $\frac{1}{2}$ $\frac{2}{4} + \frac{3}{4} = \frac{5}{4} = 1\frac{1}{4}$

   (B) $\frac{3}{4}$

   (C) $1\frac{1}{4}$

   (D) $\frac{4}{6}$

2. Each book is $\frac{7}{8}$ inch thick. How many inches high would a stack of 12 such books be?

   (F) $10\frac{1}{2}$

   (G) 12

   (H) 84

   (J) $12\frac{7}{8}$

3. A string $\frac{2}{3}$ yard long is cut into 4 pieces. Each piece is the same length. How many yards is each piece?

   (A) $2\frac{2}{3}$

   (B) $\frac{2}{3}$

   (C) $1\frac{1}{3}$

   (D) $\frac{1}{6}$

4. The Urbans had $\frac{3}{4}$ gallon of milk. One-half of this was used for dinner. How many gallons of milk were used for dinner?

   (F) $\frac{3}{4}$

   (G) $\frac{3}{8}$

   (H) $\frac{1}{2}$

   (J) $\frac{4}{6}$

5. There are 24 people at a meeting. Suppose $\frac{2}{3}$ of the people are women. How many are men?

   (A) 8

   (B) 24

   (C) 16

   (D) 12

6. Max spent $\frac{5}{6}$ hour typing. He spent $\frac{1}{6}$ hour proofreading his typing. How long did he spend typing and proofreading in all?

   (F) $\frac{4}{6}$ hour

   (G) 1 hour

   (H) $\frac{7}{6}$ hour

   (J) $\frac{5}{6}$ hour

STOP

Name _____ Date _____

Math

2.2

Multiplication and Division of Fractions

DIRECTIONS: Choose the best answer.

1. $7 \times \dfrac{1}{9}$

    Ⓐ   63

    Ⓑ $\dfrac{7}{9}$

    Ⓒ $7\dfrac{1}{9}$

    Ⓓ $\dfrac{7}{16}$

2. $\dfrac{2}{5} \times 4$

    Ⓕ $1\dfrac{3}{5}$

    Ⓖ   10

    Ⓗ $1\dfrac{4}{5}$

    Ⓙ $1\dfrac{2}{5}$

3. $\dfrac{5}{8} \times \dfrac{4}{15}$

    Ⓐ $\dfrac{2}{15}$

    Ⓑ $\dfrac{1}{6}$

    Ⓒ $\dfrac{1}{3}$

    Ⓓ $\dfrac{20}{100}$

4. $\dfrac{2}{9} \times \dfrac{7}{8}$

    Ⓕ $\dfrac{18}{56}$

    Ⓖ $\dfrac{16}{63}$

    Ⓗ $\dfrac{7}{9}$

    Ⓙ $\dfrac{7}{36}$

5. $1\dfrac{2}{3} \times 5$

    Ⓐ $2\dfrac{3}{5}$

    Ⓑ $8\dfrac{1}{3}$

    Ⓒ $5\dfrac{2}{3}$

    Ⓓ $7\dfrac{1}{3}$

6. $\dfrac{2}{3} \div \dfrac{7}{8}$

    Ⓕ $\dfrac{7}{12}$

    Ⓖ $\dfrac{16}{21}$

    Ⓗ $\dfrac{2}{3}$

    Ⓙ $\dfrac{14}{24}$

7. $\dfrac{7}{12} \div \dfrac{3}{4}$

    Ⓐ $\dfrac{21}{48}$

    Ⓑ $\dfrac{1}{3}$

    Ⓒ $\dfrac{7}{9}$

    Ⓓ $\dfrac{7}{16}$

STOP

Math
2.3

Solving Problems

DIRECTIONS: Choose the best answer.

1. There are 52 weeks in a year. Wilma works 46 weeks each year. During each week, she works 32 hours. Which number sentence below shows how many hours Wilma works in a year?

   Ⓐ $52 \times 32 = \blacksquare$

   Ⓑ $46 \times 32 = \blacksquare$

   © $32 \times 52 = \blacksquare$

   Ⓓ $(52 - 46) \times 32 = \blacksquare$

2. Angelica is helping her dad build a deck. The surface of the deck will be 12 feet wide and 14 feet long. The boards they are using can cover an area of 4 square feet each. Which of these shows how many boards they will need to cover the surface of the deck?

   Ⓕ $(12 \times 14) \div 4 = \blacksquare$

   Ⓖ $(12 \times 14) \times 4 = \blacksquare$

   Ⓗ $12 + 14 + 4 = \blacksquare$

   Ⓙ $(12 \div 14) \times 4 = \blacksquare$

3. A DVD player normally costs $119. It is on sale for $99. How much would you save if you bought two DVD players on sale?

   Ⓐ $(\$119 + \$99) \times 2 = \blacksquare$

   Ⓑ $(\$119 - \$99) \div 2 = \blacksquare$

   © $(\$119 - \$99) \times 2 = \blacksquare$

   Ⓓ $(\$119 + \$99) \div 2 = \blacksquare$

4. A carpenter has 12 pieces of wood that are each 9 feet long. He has to cut 2 feet from each piece of wood because of water damage. Which equation shows how much good wood is left?

   Ⓕ $(9 + 2) \times 12 = \blacksquare$

   Ⓖ $(12 - 2) \times 9 = \blacksquare$

   Ⓗ $(12 \times 9) - 2 = \blacksquare$

   Ⓙ $(9 - 2) \times 12 = \blacksquare$

5. A submarine is descending at a rate of 8 feet per second. How far below the surface will the submarine be in 3 minutes?

   Ⓐ 480 feet

   Ⓑ 24 feet

   © 1,440 feet

   Ⓓ 11 feet

6. The Pentagon has equal sides that each measure 276.3 meters. What is the approximate perimeter of the Pentagon?

   Ⓕ $276 \div 5$

   Ⓖ 276×5

   Ⓗ 276×4

   Ⓙ $276 + 4$

DIRECTIONS: For exercises 7–8, imagine that the temperature in Rockville at 7:00 A.M. was −7°C. By 12:00 noon, the temperature increased to 13°C, but it fell by 3°C by 6:00 P.M.

7. How much did the temperature increase between 7:00 A.M. and 12:00 noon?

   Ⓐ 6°C

   Ⓑ 20°C

   © −6°C

   Ⓓ −20°C

8. What is the average hourly temperature gain between 7:00 A.M. and 12:00 noon?

   Ⓕ −4°C

   Ⓖ 20°C

   Ⓗ 4°C

   Ⓙ −20°C

Name _____   Date _____

Math
2.4

Least Common Multiples and Greatest Common Divisors

DIRECTIONS: Use the table for the example and questions 1–5. Find the least common multiple and greatest common divisor as necessary to add and subtract the fractions.

Today's Workouts	
Kerri	$1\frac{1}{2}$ hours
Jennifer	$\frac{3}{4}$ hour
Ahmad	2 hours
Risa	$\frac{2}{3}$ hour

1. Who had a longer workout, Jennifer or Risa? How much longer?

   (A) Jennifer, $\frac{1}{12}$ hour

   (B) Jennifer, $\frac{1}{1}$ hour

   (C) Risa, $\frac{1}{12}$ hour

   (D) Risa, $\frac{1}{1}$ hour

2. How much longer was Ahmad's workout than Kerri's workout?

   (F) 1 hour

   (G) 2 hours

   (H) $3\frac{1}{2}$ hours

   (J) $\frac{1}{2}$ hour

3. Risa finished her workout just as Kerri started hers. How long did it take from the time Risa started until Kerri finished?

   (A) $1\frac{3}{5}$ hours

   (B) $2\frac{1}{6}$ hours

   (C) $\frac{5}{6}$ hour

   (D) $1\frac{5}{6}$ hours

4. Kerri and Jennifer started their workouts at the same time. Who finished first and by how much?

   (F) Kerri, $2\frac{1}{4}$ hours

   (G) Kerri, $\frac{3}{4}$ hour

   (H) Jennifer, $2\frac{1}{4}$ hours

   (J) Jennifer, $\frac{3}{4}$ hour

5. What was the total workout time for all four people on the list?

   (A) 4 hours

   (B) $4\frac{11}{12}$ hours

   (C) $3\frac{6}{9}$ hours

   (D) $4\frac{6}{9}$ hours

STOP

Name _____ Date _____

Math

2.0

For pages 92–95

Mini-Test 2

DIRECTIONS: Choose the best answer.

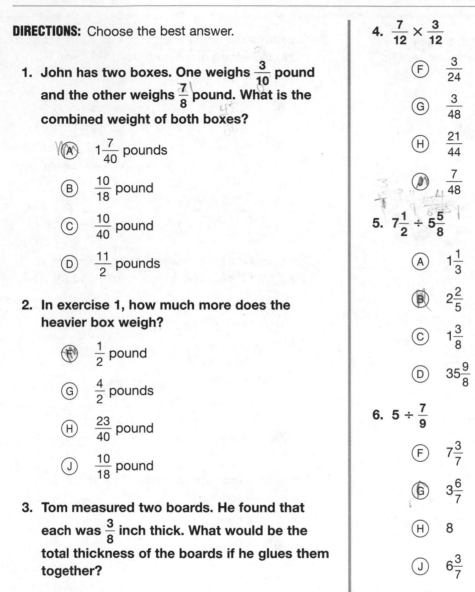

1. John has two boxes. One weighs $\frac{3}{10}$ pound and the other weighs $\frac{7}{8}$ pound. What is the combined weight of both boxes?

   (A) $1\frac{7}{40}$ pounds

   (B) $\frac{10}{18}$ pound

   (C) $\frac{10}{40}$ pound

   (D) $\frac{11}{2}$ pounds

2. In exercise 1, how much more does the heavier box weigh?

   (F) $\frac{1}{2}$ pound

   (G) $\frac{4}{2}$ pounds

   (H) $\frac{23}{40}$ pound

   (J) $\frac{10}{18}$ pound

3. Tom measured two boards. He found that each was $\frac{3}{8}$ inch thick. What would be the total thickness of the boards if he glues them together?

   (A) $\frac{3}{4}$ inch

   (B) $\frac{6}{16}$ inch

   (C) $\frac{3}{8}$ inch

   (D) $\frac{1}{2}$ inch

4. $\frac{7}{12} \times \frac{3}{12}$

   (F) $\frac{3}{24}$

   (G) $\frac{3}{48}$

   (H) $\frac{21}{44}$

   (J) $\frac{7}{48}$

5. $7\frac{1}{2} \div 5\frac{5}{8}$

   (A) $1\frac{1}{3}$

   (B) $2\frac{2}{5}$

   (C) $1\frac{3}{8}$

   (D) $35\frac{9}{8}$

6. $5 \div \frac{7}{9}$

   (F) $7\frac{3}{7}$

   (G) $3\frac{6}{7}$

   (H) 8

   (J) $6\frac{3}{7}$

How Am I Doing?

Mini-Test 1

Page 90

Number Correct

8–9 answers correct	**Great Job!** Move on to the section test on page 98.
5–7 answers correct	**You're almost there!** But you still need a little practice. Review practice pages 86–89 before moving on to the section test on page 98.
0–4 answers correct	**Oops!** Time to review what you have learned and try again. Review the practice section on pages 86–89. Then retake the test on page 90. Now move on to the section test on page 98.

Mini-Test 2

Page 96

Number Correct

6 answers correct	**Awesome!** Move on to the section test on page 98.
4–5 answers correct	**You're almost there!** But you still need a little practice. Review practice pages 92–95 before moving on to the section test on page 98.
0–3 answers correct	**Oops!** Time to review what you have learned and try again. Review the practice section on pages 92–95. Then retake the test on page 96. Now move on to the section test on page 98.

Final Number Sense Test
for pages 86–96

DIRECTIONS: Choose the best answer.

1. How many of the following fractions are greater than $\frac{2}{3}$?

$$\frac{2}{5}, \frac{3}{4}, \frac{5}{8}, \frac{6}{7}, \frac{4}{9}, \frac{8}{19}$$

   (A) 2
   (B) 1
   (C) 5
   (D) 4

2. A sales tax of 5% is charged on all purchases. What is the sales tax on a purchase of $78?

   (F) $390.00
   (G) $39.00
   (H) $3.90
   (J) $0.39

3. Charge-account customers must pay a finance charge of 21% of their unpaid balance. What is the finance charge to a customer who has an unpaid balance of $82?

   (A) $17.22
   (B) $21.00
   (C) $1.72
   (D) $82.00

4. $\frac{2.3}{4.6} = \frac{n}{6.2}$

   (F) 3.2
   (G) 3.1
   (H) 32
   (J) 31

5. $\frac{7}{49} = \frac{12}{n}$

   (A) 54
   (B) 144
   (C) 7
   (D) 84

6. $\frac{30}{12} = \frac{n}{40}$

   (F) 100
   (G) 50
   (H) 18
   (J) 120

7. $\frac{66}{n} = \frac{22}{2}$

   (A) 33
   (B) 11
   (C) 6
   (D) 3

8. Mrs. Hartman's sixth grade class has twenty-four students. There are 18 girls. What is the ratio of girls to total students?

   (F) $\frac{3}{4}$
   (G) $\frac{1}{6}$
   (H) $\frac{1}{3}$
   (J) $\frac{1}{2}$

9. Grant's family drove 180 miles in 3 hours. What was their mile-per-hour ratio?

   (A) 180 miles per hour
   (B) 3 miles per hour
   (C) 60 miles per hour
   (D) 20 miles per hour

10. Marty made a base hit once out of four times at bat. What was his batting average?

   (F) 4:1
   (G) 1:4
   (H) 1
   (J) 4

GO

11. A sock drawer has 5 brown pairs of socks, 3 red pairs of socks, and 6 blue pairs of socks. Which of the following does not show the ratio of red to blue?

Ⓐ $\frac{3}{6}$

Ⓑ 3:6

Ⓒ 1:3

Ⓓ 3 to 6

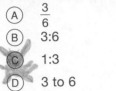

12. Which of these groups of numbers is in order from least to greatest?

Ⓕ 16.089, 14.876, 18.999, 22.800

Ⓖ 22.888, 22.989, 22.897, 23.001

Ⓗ 12.954, 13.656, 13.875, 15.877

Ⓙ 12.443, 11.339, 11.123, 10.458

13. Which group of numbers is ordered from least to greatest?

Ⓐ −18.29, −12.89, −98.21, −29.81

Ⓑ −12.47, −12.74, −41.27, −72.14

Ⓒ −68.24, −86.42, −64.28, −48.26

Ⓓ −59.73, −57.93, −53.79, −39.75

14. Marlena and Zander went out for dinner. Their bill was $45.75. They want to leave a 15% tip rounded up to the nearest dollar. How much should they leave?

Ⓕ $6.86

Ⓖ $6.00

Ⓗ $7.00

Ⓙ $6.90

15. Shawna deposited $500 into a savings account that earned her 2.5% per year through simple compound interest. How much money in total did she have after one year?

Ⓐ $2.50

Ⓑ $12.50

Ⓒ $502.50

Ⓓ $512.50

16. The boys can walk $3\frac{1}{2}$ miles in 1 hour. At that rate, how many miles could the boys walk in $1\frac{1}{6}$ hours?

Ⓕ $3\frac{1}{2}$ miles

Ⓖ $1\frac{1}{6}$ miles

Ⓗ $4\frac{1}{12}$ miles

Ⓙ $4\frac{1}{2}$ miles

17. It rained $\frac{3}{4}$ inch yesterday and $\frac{3}{10}$ inch today. How much more did it rain yesterday?

Ⓐ $\frac{3}{4}$ inch

Ⓑ $\frac{3}{10}$ inch

Ⓒ $1\frac{1}{20}$ inches

Ⓓ $\frac{9}{20}$ inch

18. Maranda read $\frac{3}{5}$ hour in the morning and $\frac{1}{2}$ hour in the afternoon. How many hours did she read total?

Ⓕ $\frac{3}{5}$ hour

Ⓖ $1\frac{1}{10}$ hours

Ⓗ $\frac{1}{2}$ hour

Ⓙ $\frac{1}{10}$ hour

19. Karyln works $1\frac{1}{2}$ hours each day. How many days will it take her to work 15 hours?

Ⓐ 10 days

Ⓑ 15 days

Ⓒ 8 days

Ⓓ $9\frac{1}{2}$ days

GO ▷

20. An unopened box of cereal weighed $\frac{15}{16}$ pound. Mother used $\frac{1}{3}$ pound of cereal from the box. How much cereal remains in the box?

   F $1\frac{1}{3}$ pounds

   G $\frac{29}{48}$ pound

   H $\frac{1}{3}$ pound

   J $\frac{1}{2}$ pound

21. A television show has just begun and will last $\frac{5}{6}$ hour. After $\frac{4}{7}$ hour, what part of an hour remains of the television show?

   A $\frac{4}{7}$ hour

   B $1\frac{17}{42}$ hours

   C $\frac{5}{6}$ hour

   D $\frac{11}{42}$ hour

22. Tess jogged $\frac{4}{5}$ hour before work. That same day she jogged $\frac{3}{4}$ hour after work. How long did she jog in all that day?

   F $1\frac{11}{20}$ hours

   G $\frac{1}{20}$ hour

   H $\frac{4}{5}$ hour

   J $\frac{3}{4}$ hour

23. While Julian was recovering from the flu, his temperature dropped 1° steadily each hour for 3 hours. What was the total change?

   A −1°

   B 1°

   C −3°

   D 3°

24. Hector's neighborhood is having a rummage sale. The expenses are $10 for flyers, $35 for advertising, and $50 for table rentals. They made a total of $525. How much profit did they make?

   F $620

   G $430

   H $525

   J $95

25. In exercise 24, there were 5 families taking part in the rummage sale. How much does each family get?

   A $105

   B $124

   C $19

   D $86

26. Fifty percent of the people questioned in a sales survey indicated a preference for Brand X. There were 7,520 people questioned. How many of the people questioned preferred Brand X?

   F 3,760

   G 7,520

   H 50

   J 3,500

27. During the sale Mr. Hansen purchased a coat for 60% off the regular price. The coat normally sold for $220. How much money did he save by buying the coat on sale?

   A $60

   B $220

   C $132

   D $88

GO

28. $\frac{7}{3} \times \frac{6}{9}$

  (F) $\frac{2}{27}$

  (G) $\frac{1}{9}$

  (H) $1\frac{5}{9}$

  (J) $\frac{13}{27}$

29. $12 \times \frac{4}{5}$

  (A) $9\frac{2}{8}$

  (B) $8\frac{2}{5}$

  (C) $9\frac{4}{5}$

  (D) $9\frac{3}{5}$

30. $1\frac{1}{12} \times \frac{3}{8}$

  (F) $\frac{31}{32}$

  (G) $\frac{1}{4}$

  (H) $\frac{3}{32}$

  (J) $\frac{13}{32}$

31. $\frac{8}{9} \div \frac{1}{4}$

  (A) $5\frac{1}{3}$

  (B) $\frac{1}{36}$

  (C) $3\frac{5}{9}$

  (D) $\frac{2}{9}$

32. $\frac{3}{20} \div \frac{9}{10}$

  (F) $\frac{1}{6}$

  (G) $\frac{2}{9}$

  (H) $1\frac{2}{7}$

  (J) $\frac{9}{10}$

33. $1\frac{11}{15} \div 1\frac{19}{20}$

  (A) $\frac{3}{5}$

  (B) $\frac{8}{9}$

  (C) $\frac{1}{7}$

  (D) $\frac{8}{13}$

34. Angelina read $\frac{3}{5}$ hour in the morning and $\frac{1}{2}$ hour in the evening. How much longer did she read in the morning than in the evening?

  (F) $\frac{3}{5}$ hour

  (G) $1\frac{1}{10}$ hours

  (H) $\frac{1}{10}$ hour

  (J) $\frac{1}{2}$ hour

STOP

Name _____ Date _____

Number Sense Test
Answer Sheet

1 Ⓐ Ⓑ Ⓒ Ⓓ
2 Ⓕ Ⓖ Ⓗ Ⓙ
3 Ⓐ Ⓑ Ⓒ Ⓓ
4 Ⓕ Ⓖ Ⓗ Ⓙ
5 Ⓐ Ⓑ Ⓒ Ⓓ
6 Ⓕ Ⓖ Ⓗ Ⓙ
7 Ⓐ Ⓑ Ⓒ Ⓓ
8 Ⓕ Ⓖ Ⓗ Ⓙ
9 Ⓐ Ⓑ Ⓒ Ⓓ
10 Ⓕ Ⓖ Ⓗ Ⓙ

11 Ⓐ Ⓑ Ⓒ Ⓓ
12 Ⓕ Ⓖ Ⓗ Ⓙ
13 Ⓐ Ⓑ Ⓒ Ⓓ
14 Ⓕ Ⓖ Ⓗ Ⓙ
15 Ⓐ Ⓑ Ⓒ Ⓓ
16 Ⓕ Ⓖ Ⓗ Ⓙ
17 Ⓐ Ⓑ Ⓒ Ⓓ
18 Ⓕ Ⓖ Ⓗ Ⓙ
19 Ⓐ Ⓑ Ⓒ Ⓓ
20 Ⓕ Ⓖ Ⓗ Ⓙ

21 Ⓐ Ⓑ Ⓒ Ⓓ
22 Ⓕ Ⓖ Ⓗ Ⓙ
23 Ⓐ Ⓑ Ⓒ Ⓓ
24 Ⓕ Ⓖ Ⓗ Ⓙ
25 Ⓐ Ⓑ Ⓒ Ⓓ
26 Ⓕ Ⓖ Ⓗ Ⓙ
27 Ⓐ Ⓑ Ⓒ Ⓓ
28 Ⓕ Ⓖ Ⓗ Ⓙ
29 Ⓐ Ⓑ Ⓒ Ⓓ
30 Ⓕ Ⓖ Ⓗ Ⓙ

31 Ⓐ Ⓑ Ⓒ Ⓓ
32 Ⓕ Ⓖ Ⓗ Ⓙ
33 Ⓐ Ⓑ Ⓒ Ⓓ
34 Ⓕ Ⓖ Ⓗ Ⓙ

Algebra and Functions Standards

1.0 Students write verbal expressions and sentences as algebraic expressions and equations; they evaluate algebraic expressions, solve simple linear equations, and graph and interpret their results:

1.1 Write and solve one-step linear equations in one variable. *(See page 104.)*

What it means:
- An example of a one-step linear equation is $32 = 15 + x$.

1.2 Write and evaluate an algebraic expression for a given situation, using up to three variables. *(See page 105.)*

1.3 Apply algebraic order of operations and the commutative, associative, and distributive properties to evaluate expressions; and justify each step in the process. *(See page 106.)*

1.4 Solve problems manually by using the correct order of operations or by using a scientific calculator. *(See page 107.)*

Solving Equations

DIRECTIONS: Choose the best answer.

1. **What is the value of z in the equation 12 × z = 144?**
   - (A) 8
   - (B) 12
   - (C) 122
   - (D) 11

2. **What is the value of x if 54 ÷ x = 9?**
   - (F) 7
   - (G) 6
   - (H) 63
   - (J) 45

3. **What is the value of r if 17 × r = 68?**
   - (A) 51
   - (B) 4
   - (C) 85
   - (D) 6

4. **What is the value of a in the equation (7 × a) − 9 = 54?**
   - (F) 8
   - (G) 7
   - (H) 5
   - (J) 9

5. **If z + 8 = 31, then z =**
   - (A) 39
   - (B) 23
   - (C) 22
   - (D) 4

6. **Your uncle bought 375 feet of wire fencing. He put up 325 feet today and saved the rest for tomorrow. Which equation shows how many feet of fencing he has left?**
   - (F) 375 + f = 325
   - (G) 375 − 325 = f
   - (H) f = 375 + 325
   - (J) 375 − f = 325

7. **If 27 students each brought in 6 cookies, which equation shows how many cookies they brought in all?**
   - (A) 27 + 6 = c
   - (B) 27 × 6 = c
   - (C) 27 − 6 = c
   - (D) 27 ÷ 6 = c

8. **Which equation shows the total attendance at the Science Fair if 67 girls and 59 boys attended?**
   - (F) 67 − 59 = a
   - (G) 67 + 59 = a
   - (H) 67 ÷ 59 = a
   - (J) 67 × 59 = a

9. **Sergio spent $3.80 on heavy-duty string for his project. He bought 20 feet of string. Which equation could you use to find out the price per foot of the string?**
   - (A) $3.80 + 20 = s
   - (B) $3.80 − 20 = s
   - (C) $3.80 × 20 = s
   - (D) $3.80 ÷ 20 = s

STOP

Name _____ Date _____

Algebraic Expressions

Clue — Look for key words, numbers, and figures in each problem, and be sure you perform the correct operation.

DIRECTIONS: Choose the best answer.

1. **A desk normally costs $129. It is on sale for $99. How much would you save if you bought 2 desks on sale?**

   Ⓐ ($129 + $99) × 2 = s

   Ⓑ ($129 − $99) ÷ 2 = s

   Ⓒ ($129 − $99) × 2 = s

   Ⓓ ($129 + $99) ÷ 2 = s

2. **The highway department uses 6 gallons of paint for every 10 blocks of highway stripe. How many gallons will be needed for 250 blocks of highway stripe?**

   Ⓕ (6 × 10) + 250 = g

   Ⓖ 250 − (10 ÷ 6) = g

   Ⓗ 250 × 10 × 6 = g

   Ⓙ (250 ÷ 10) × 6 = g

3. **A hiker started out with 48 ounces of water. She drank 9 ounces of water after hiking 5 miles and 16 more when she reached mile marker 8. How many ounces of water did she have left?**

   Ⓐ 48 − (9 + 16) = w

   Ⓑ 48 + (9 − 16) = w

   Ⓒ (16 − 9) + 48 = w

   Ⓓ 48 + (9 + 16) = w

4. **Evaluate $2a − 3b + 4c$, if $a = 4$, $b = 3$, and $c = 2$.**

   Ⓕ 25

   Ⓖ 38

   Ⓗ 7

   Ⓙ 12

5. **Evaluate $5g + 2h$, if $g = 1$ and $h = 4$.**

   Ⓐ 13

   Ⓑ 28

   Ⓒ 22

   Ⓓ 7

6. **A barrel is 36 inches from top to bottom. The water in the barrel is $12\frac{1}{2}$ inches deep. How much space is there from the surface of the water to the top of the barrel?**

   Ⓕ $s = 36 ÷ 12\frac{1}{2}$

   Ⓖ $s = 36 × 12\frac{1}{2}$

   Ⓗ $s = 36 − 12\frac{1}{2}$

   Ⓙ $s = 36 + 12\frac{1}{2}$

For exercise 7 use the following information. The base of Sandy Mountain is 5,400 feet above sea level. The top of the mountain is 10,700 feet above sea level. A trail runs from the base of the mountain to the top. The trail is 8 miles long, and it takes about 5 hours to hike from the base of the mountain to the top.

7. **Which of the following equations could be used to determine the vertical distance from the base of the mountain to the top?**

   Ⓐ $t − b = 5,300$

   Ⓑ $t + b = 16,100$

   Ⓒ $t × b = 57,780,000$

   Ⓓ $t ÷ b = 1.98$

1.3

Number Properties

Example:

Solve the equation for *x*. $7x(2 + 5) = x + 23$

- (A) 11
- (B) 24
- (C) 26
- (D) 13

Answer: (C)

DIRECTIONS: Choose the best answer.

1. **Which statement is true if *b* is a whole number?**

   (A) If $b - 8 = 16$, then $8 + b = 16$.

   (B) If $8 \times b = 16$, then $16 \div b = 8$.

   (C) If $8 \div b = 16$, then $16 \times 8 = b$.

   (D) If $8 + b = 16$, then $16 + 8 = b$.

2. $4 \times 35 = 4 \times (z + 5)$

   (F) $z = 35$

   (G) $z = 30$

   (H) $z = 3$

   (J) $z = 38$

3. **What value does *c* have in the equation $8 \times 7 = (6 \times 6) + (4 \times c)$?**

   (A) 4

   (B) 6

   (C) 5

   (D) 7

4. **If $6 < f$ and $f < g$, what should replace the square in $6 \blacksquare g$?**

   (F) $<$

   (G) $>$

   (H) $-$

   (J) $=$

5. **Which is another name for 45?**

   (A) $(4 \times 5) + 10$

   (B) $4 + (5 \times 1)$

   (C) $51 - (3 \times 2)$

   (D) $(3 \times 3) \times 6$

6. **Which value of m solves the equation $4 \times (3 + 5) = m + 17$?**

   (F) 11

   (G) 6

   (H) 0

   (J) 15

7. **A plane has six rows of 20 seats. Passengers are in 92 seats. How many seats are empty?**

   (A) $(6 \times 20) \div 92 = e$

   (B) $(6 \times 20) - 92 = e$

   (C) $92 \times (6 \times 20) = e$

   (D) $92 + (6 \times 20) = e$

8. **Which is not another name for 81?**

   (F) $(8 \times 9) + 9$

   (G) 3^4

   (H) $3^2 + 3^2$

   (J) 27×3

Algebra and Functions

Solving Problems

DIRECTIONS: Choose the best answer.

1. You helped your mom plant 40 tulip bulbs in the fall. In the spring, 10 of the tulips did not come up at all, and $\frac{1}{3}$ of the rest had yellow flowers. Which of the equations shows how to find the number of tulips that had yellow flowers?

   (A) $40 - 10 = \frac{1}{3} \times t$

   (B) $\frac{1}{3} \times (40 - 10) = t$

   (C) $(\frac{1}{3} \times 40) - 10 = t$

   (D) $(\frac{1}{3} \times 10) = t$

2. A store is open for 12 hours a day. Each hour, an average of 15 customers comes into the store. How many customers come into the store in a day?

   (F) $15 \times 24 = c$
   (G) $12 + 15 = c$
   (H) $12 \times 15 = c$
   (J) $24 \div 12 = c$

3. $2 + 4 \times 8 =$

   (A) 48
   (B) 64
   (C) 34
   (D) 14

4. $15 - 11 + 4 - 3 =$

   (F) 5
   (G) -32
   (H) -3
   (J) 7

5. $48 - (6 + 3) \times 4 =$

   (A) 180
   (B) 54
   (C) 12
   (D) 156

6. $13 \times 9 - 5 =$

   (F) 52
   (G) 112
   (H) 17
   (J) 27

7. $18 - 2 \times 5 - 1 =$

   (A) 79
   (B) 64
   (C) 7
   (D) 9

8. $34 + (16 - 5) \times 2 =$

   (F) 56
   (G) 90
   (H) 40
   (J) 80

9. $76 \div 19 \times 4 =$

   (A) 1
   (B) 16
   (C) 19
   (D) 76

10. $121 \div 11 + 4 \times 8 =$

   (F) 120
   (G) 64
   (H) 1
   (J) 43

Math

1.0

For pages 104–107

Mini-Test 1

Algebra and Functions

DIRECTIONS: Choose the best answer.

1. For your science project, you planted 50 flower seeds. You found that 20 of the seeds didn't grow at all, and $\frac{2}{3}$ of the rest had red flowers. Which of the equations show how to find the number of plants that had red flowers?

   (A) $50 - 20 = \frac{2}{3} \times r$

   (B) $\frac{2}{3} \times (50 - 20) = r$

   (C) $(\frac{2}{3} \times 50) - 20 = r$

   (D) $(\frac{2}{3} \times 20) = r$

2. A pair of sunglasses costs $12.95 and a hat costs $7.25. How much change would you receive if you bought a pair of glasses and paid for the glasses with a $20 bill?

   (F) $20 - g = \$7.25$

   (G) $(\$12.95 + \$7.25) - \$20 = g$

   (H) $\$20 - (\$12.95 + \$7.25) = g$

   (J) $\$20 - \$12.95 = g$

3. The Perez family is planning next year's vacation. They want to save $20 each week for 52 weeks. The three children in the family will each give $1 a week, Mrs. Perez will give $10, and Mr. Perez will give the rest. How much money will they have for vacation?

   (A) $72

   (B) $2,600

   (C) $140

   (D) $1,040

4. Evaluate $3x - y$, if $x = 4$ and $y = 1$.

   (F) 11

   (G) 12

   (H) 6

   (J) 9

5. Diane makes $5.50 an hour. If Diane stays on the job for 6 months, she will receive a $0.50 an hour raise. If she stays 6 more months, she will receive another raise of $0.75. How much will Diane earn per hour if she stays on the job for 12 months?

   (A) $1.25

   (B) $6.00

   (C) $6.75

   (D) $7.25

6. A can of soup at the market costs $0.69, a loaf of bread costs $1.19, and a bunch of bananas is $1.25. During a sale, the price of each of the items was reduced by $0.10. How much would it cost to buy all three items during the sale?

   (F) $3.13

   (G) $3.03

   (H) $2.38

   (J) $2.83

7. $72 \div 12 - 4$

   (A) 2

   (B) 9

   (C) 6

   (D) 10

108

Algebra and Functions Standards

2.0 Students analyze and use tables, graphs, and rules to solve problems involving rates and proportions:

2.1 Convert one unit of measurement to another (e.g., from feet to miles, from centimeters to inches). *(See page 110.)*

2.2 Demonstrate an understanding that rate is a measure of one quantity per unit value of another quantity. *(See page 111.)*

2.3 Solve problems involving rates, average speed, distance, and time. *(See page 112.)*

Name _____   Date _____

Converting Units of Measurement

DIRECTIONS: Choose the best answer.

1. **Anthony's trampoline is about 3 yards across. About how many inches across is his trampoline?**

   (A) 108 inches

   (B) 36 inches

   (C) 54 inches

   (D) 30 inches

2. **How many quarts are in 6 gallons?**

   (F) 48

   (G) 24

   (H) 16

   (J) 12

3. **130 inches is _____.**

   (A) exactly 10 feet

   (B) more than 3 yards

   (C) between 9 and 10 feet

   (D) less than 3 yards

4. **How many milliliters are equal to 2.81 liters?**

   (F) 28.10 milliliters

   (G) 2810.0 milliliters

   (H) 2000.81 milliliters

   (J) 0.00281 milliliters

5. **Margo's bed is about 2 yards long. About how many inches long is her bed?**

   (A) 24 inches

   (B) 72 inches

   (C) 6 inches

   (D) 36 inches

6. **Cindy is building a doghouse. It will be 32 inches high. Another way to describe the height of the doghouse is to say it is _____.**

   (F) a little more than 1 yard high

   (G) a little less than 2 feet high

   (H) a little less than 1 yard high

   (J) a little more than 4 feet high

7. **How many pints are in 5 quarts?**

   (A) 10

   (B) 7

   (C) 20

   (D) 15

8. **Paul's fishing rod is 1.5 meters long. How many millimeters long is it?**

   (F) 150

   (G) 150,000

   (H) 15,000

   (J) 1,500

9. **100 inches is _____.**

   (A) more than 3 yards

   (B) between 8 and 9 feet

   (C) exactly 10 feet

   (D) less than 2 yards

10. **The top of a doorway is 84 inches above the floor. What is the height of the doorway in feet?**

    (F) 84

    (G) $2\frac{1}{3}$

    (H) 7

    (J) 28

Math

2.2

Rates

Example:

What is 160 miles on 5 gallons of gasoline as a rate?

- (A) 50 miles per gallon
- (B) 32 miles per gallon
- (C) 155 miles per gallon
- (D) 12 miles per gallon

Answer: (B)

DIRECTIONS: Choose the best answer.

1. **What is 8 apples for $2 as a rate?**
   - (A) $0.50 per apple
   - (B) $0.75 per apple
   - (C) $0.25 per apple
   - (D) $0.10 per apple

2. **What is 400 kilometers in 5 hours as a rate?**
   - (F) 200 kilometers per hour
   - (G) 405 kilometers per hour
   - (H) 100 kilometers per hour
   - (J) 80 kilometers per hour

3. **Tim drove 558 miles in 9 hours. What was his rate?**
   - (A) 62 miles per hour
   - (B) 60 miles per hour
   - (C) 65 miles per hour
   - (D) 558 miles per hour

4. **The school has 2 student council representatives for every 28 students. What is the representative rate?**
   - (F) 28 students per representative
   - (G) 12 students per representative
   - (H) 14 students per representative
   - (J) 2 students per representative

5. **Karen can type 105 words in 3 minutes. What is her typing rate?**
   - (A) 33 words per minute
   - (B) 35 words per minute
   - (C) 40 words per minute
   - (D) 105 words per minute

6. **The Paices drove 2,800 miles in 7 days. What was their rate per day?**
   - (F) 400 miles per day
   - (G) 4,000 miles per day
   - (H) 7 miles per day
   - (J) 280 miles per day

7. **Victoria paid $38 for 2 sweaters. How much was it for each sweater?**
   - (A) $17 per sweater
   - (B) $19 per sweater
   - (C) $21 per sweater
   - (D) $38 per sweater

8. **Pedro saved $375 in 5 years. How much did he save per year?**
   - (F) $85 per year
   - (G) $375 per year
   - (H) $75 per year
   - (J) $5 per year

STOP

Name _____   Date _____

Algebra and Functions

Rate, Speed, Distance, and Time

Clue When working with word problems, cross out any extra information and draw a picture to help organize the given information. Keep track of what you know and what you want to know.

DIRECTIONS: Draw pictures to help answer the following questions.

1. Charlene is cycling around a track at 15 miles per hour. Chloe starts at the same time in the same direction, but only goes 12 miles per hour. How many minutes after they start will Charlene pass Chloe if the track is $\frac{1}{2}$ mile long?

_____

2. How long does it take Chuck to circle the same track once at the rate of 3 miles per hour?

_____

3. How fast would Chas have to walk around a one-mile track in order to circle it once every twenty minutes?

_____

4. Stan has asked his friend Robin for a potion to turn them and their friend Barb into birds for a trip to Diamond Alley. Diamond Alley is 9 miles away and a dose of Robin's potion lasts 50 minutes. They only have enough potion for one dose each. If they can go 24 miles an hour as birds, and they start at 4:30 P.M., can they get to Diamond Alley and back to school again before the potion runs out at 5:20 P.M.? If so, how much time will they be able to spend in the Alley?

_____

Math

2.0

For pages 110–112

DIRECTIONS: Choose the best answer.

1. The distance along the foul line from home plate to the right field fence is 336 feet. What is this distance in yards?

(A) 336

(B) 112

(C) $9\frac{1}{3}$

(D) 28

2. A snake is 4 feet 3 inches long. What is the length of the snake in inches?

(F) 51 inches

(G) 48 inches

(H) 45 inches

(J) $1\frac{1}{3}$ inches

3. There are 8,000 liters of water in a pool. How many kiloliters of water are in that pool?

(A) 8,000 kL

(B) 800 kL

(C) 80 kL

(D) 8 kL

4. Felipe had 72 hits in 24 baseball games. What was his hitting rate?

(F) 3 hits per game

(G) 12 hits per game

(H) 48 hits per game

(J) 96 hits per game

5. Chelsea's car used 12 gallons of gasoline to drive 336 miles. What was her miles-to-gallon rate?

(A) 28 miles per gallon

(B) 26 miles per gallon

(C) 4,032 miles per gallon

(D) 324 miles per gallon

6. Alfonso drove the first 360 miles of his trip in 8 hours. What is his rate of speed?

(F) 90 miles per hour

(G) 60 miles per hour

(H) 55 miles per hour

(J) 45 miles per hour

7. Steven ran a 12-mile race at an average speed of 8 miles per hour. If Adam ran the same race at an average speed of 6 miles per hour, how many minutes longer than Steve did Adam take to complete the race?

(A) 15 minutes

(B) $1\frac{1}{2}$ hour

(C) 30 minutes

(D) 2 hours

8. If you travel one mile in 45 seconds, how fast are you driving?

(F) 45 miles per hour

(G) 80 miles per hour

(H) $1\frac{1}{3}$ miles per hour

(J) 50 miles per hour

9. Becky traveled 635 kilometers at 57 kilometers per hour. How long did it take her?

(A) approximately 11 hours

(B) approximately 578 hours

(C) approximately 22 hours

(D) approximately 10 hours

10. Each bottle holds 40 milliliters of vanilla. How many such bottles can be filled from 1 liter of vanilla?

(A) 25

(B) 40

(C) 0.025

(D) 2.5

STOP

Algebra and Functions Standards

3.0 Students investigate geometric patterns and describe them algebraically:

3.1 Use variables in expressions describing geometric quantities (e.g., $P = 2w + 2\ell$, $A = \frac{1}{2}bh$, $C = \pi d$ — the formulas for the perimeter of a rectangle, the area of a triangle, and the circumference of a circle, respectively). *(See page 115.)*

3.2 Express in symbolic form simple relationships arising from geometry. *(See page 116.)*

What it means:

- There are many symbols used in naming figures in geometry. For example, a segment is named $\overline{AB}$. A ray is named $\overrightarrow{AB}$, a line is named $\overleftrightarrow{AB}$, and an angle is $\angle A$.

Math
3.1

Algebra and Functions

Using Variables

Example:

Find A = ℓ × w, if ℓ = 12 inches and w = 14 inches.

- (A) 2 in^2
- (B) 168 in^2
- (C) 26 in^2
- (D) 1.2 in^2

Answer: (B)

DIRECTIONS: Choose the best answer.

1. Find A = $\frac{1}{2}$ bh, if b = 7 feet and h = 4 feet.
   - (A) 14 ft^2
   - (B) 28 ft^2
   - (C) 3.5 ft^2
   - (D) 7.5 ft^2

2. Find P = 2w + 2ℓ, if w = 36 centimeters and ℓ = 23 centimeters.
   - (F) 61 cm
   - (G) 59 cm
   - (H) 118 cm
   - (J) 236 cm

3. Find C = πd, if d = 5 meters.
   - (A) 15.7 m
   - (B) 10 m
   - (C) 15 m
   - (D) 78.5 m

4. Find A = πr^2, if r = 3 kilometers.
   - (F) 9.42 km^2
   - (G) 18.84 km^2
   - (H) 56.52 km^2
   - (J) 28.26 km^2

5. Find A = ℓ × w, if ℓ = 42 miles and w = 18 miles.
   - (A) $2\frac{1}{3}$ mi^2
   - (B) 756 mi^2
   - (C) 60 mi^2
   - (D) 24 mi^2

6. Find P = 2w + 2ℓ, if w = 8 inches and ℓ = 12 inches.
   - (F) 40 in.
   - (G) 20 in.
   - (H) 80 in.
   - (J) 30 in.

7. Find A = $\frac{1}{2}$ bh, if b = 4.2 meters and h = 6.5 meters.
   - (A) 2.1 m^2
   - (B) 54.6 m^2
   - (C) 27.3 m^2
   - (D) 13.65 m^2

8. Find C = πd, if d = 9 feet.
   - (F) 28.26 ft
   - (G) 9.42 ft
   - (H) 254.34 ft
   - (J) 14.13 ft

STOP

Geometric Relationships

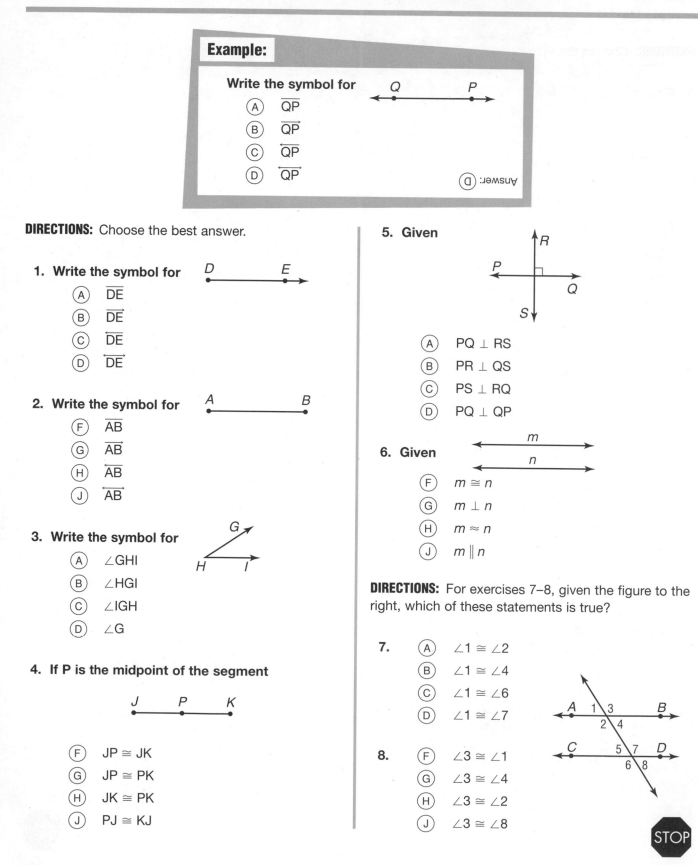

Example:

Write the symbol for

Q   P

(A) $\overline{QP}$

(B) $\overrightarrow{QP}$

(C) $\overrightarrow{QP}$

(D) $\overleftrightarrow{QP}$

Answer: (D)

DIRECTIONS: Choose the best answer.

1. **Write the symbol for**

D   E

(A) $\overline{DE}$

(B) $\overrightarrow{DE}$

(C) $\overline{DE}$

(D) $\overleftrightarrow{DE}$

2. **Write the symbol for**

A   B

(F) $\overline{AB}$

(G) $\overrightarrow{AB}$

(H) $\overleftrightarrow{AB}$

(J) $\overrightarrow{AB}$

3. **Write the symbol for**

G
H   I

(A) $\angle GHI$

(B) $\angle HGI$

(C) $\angle IGH$

(D) $\angle G$

4. **If P is the midpoint of the segment**

J   P   K

(F) $JP \cong JK$

(G) $JP \cong PK$

(H) $JK \cong PK$

(J) $PJ \cong KJ$

5. **Given**

R
P
Q
S

(A) $PQ \perp RS$

(B) $PR \perp QS$

(C) $PS \perp RQ$

(D) $PQ \perp QP$

6. **Given**

m
n

(F) $m \cong n$

(G) $m \perp n$

(H) $m \approx n$

(J) $m \parallel n$

DIRECTIONS: For exercises 7–8, given the figure to the right, which of these statements is true?

7. (A) $\angle 1 \cong \angle 2$

(B) $\angle 1 \cong \angle 4$

(C) $\angle 1 \cong \angle 6$

(D) $\angle 1 \cong \angle 7$

8. (F) $\angle 3 \cong \angle 1$

(G) $\angle 3 \cong \angle 4$

(H) $\angle 3 \cong \angle 2$

(J) $\angle 3 \cong \angle 8$

A 1 3   B
2 4
C   5 7 D
6 8

STOP

Math

Algebra and Functions

3.0

For pages 115–116

Mini-Test 3

DIRECTIONS: Choose the best answer. Use 3.14 for π.

1. Find $P = 2w + 2\ell$, if $w = 10$ and $\ell = 7$.

   (A) 17

   (B) 34

   (C) 27

   (D) 24

2. Find $A = \frac{1}{2}bh$, if $b = 15$ and $h = 15$.

   (F) 30 units^2

   (G) 60 units^2

   (H) 225 units^2

   (J) 112.5 units^2

3. Find $A = \ell \times w$, if $\ell = 13$ and $w = 8$.

   (A) 104 units^2

   (B) 52 units^2

   (C) 21 units^2

   (D) 42 units^2

4. Find $C = \pi d$, if $d = 7$.

   (F) 5.5

   (G) 10.99

   (H) 21.98

   (J) 38.47

5. Find $A = \pi r^2$, if $r = 5$.

   (A) 39.3 units^2

   (B) 78.5 units^2

   (C) 31.4 units^2

   (D) 15.7 units^2

6. Find $P = 2w + 2\ell$, if $w = 8.1$ and $\ell = 11.3$.

   (F) 16.2

   (G) 22.3

   (H) 38.8

   (J) 91.5

7. Name the angle.

   (A) $\angle$D

   (B) $\angle$DEF

   (C) $\angle$F

   (D) $\angle$EDF

8. Name the figure.

   (F) $\overline{HJ}$

   (G) $\overrightarrow{HJ}$

   (H) $\overleftrightarrow{HJ}$

   (J) $\overrightarrow{HJ}$

DIRECTIONS: For exercises 9–10, given the figure to the right, which of these statements is true?

9. (A) $\overline{FG} \parallel \overline{HJ}$

   (B) $\overline{FH} \parallel \overline{GJ}$

   (C) $1 \parallel 5$

   (D) $\overline{FJ} \parallel \overline{GH}$

10. (F) $\angle 5 \cong \angle 2$

    (G) $\angle 5 \cong \angle 4$

    (H) $\angle 5 \cong \angle 6$

    (J) $\angle 5 \cong \angle 7$

How Am I Doing?

Mini-Test 1 Page 108 **Number Correct**	**7** answers correct	**Great Job!** Move on to the section test on page 119.
	5–6 answers correct	**You're almost there!** But you still need a little practice. Review practice pages 104–107 before moving on to the section test on page 119.
	0–4 answers correct	**Oops!** Time to review what you have learned and try again. Review the practice section on pages 104–107. Then retake the test on page 108. Now move on to the section test on page 119.
Mini-Test 2 Page 113 **Number Correct**	**9–10** answers correct	**Awesome!** Move on to the section test on page 119.
	6–8 answers correct	**You're almost there!** But you still need a little practice. Review practice pages 110–112 before moving on to the section test on page 119.
	0–5 answers correct	**Oops!** Time to review what you have learned and try again. Review the practice section on pages 110–112. Then retake the test on page 113. Now move on to the section test on page 119.
Mini-Test 3 Page 117 **Number Correct**	**9–10** answers correct	**Great Job!** Move on to the section test on page 119.
	6–8 answers correct	**You're almost there!** But you still need a little practice. Review practice pages 115–116 before moving on to the section test on page 119.
	0–5 answers correct	**Oops!** Time to review what you have learned and try again. Review the practice section on pages 115–116. Then retake the test on page 117. Now move on to the section test on page 119.

Name _____   Date _____

Final Algebra and Functions Test
for pages 104–117

DIRECTIONS: Choose the best answer.

1. Which statement is true if *n* is a whole number?

   Ⓐ If $n - 9 = 18$, then $9 + n = 18$.

   Ⓑ If $9 + n = 18$, then $9 + 18 = n$.

   Ⓒ If $9 \times n = 18$, then $18 \div n = 9$.

   Ⓓ If $9 \div n = 18$, then $18 \times 9 = n$.

2. What is the value of *t* if $56 \div t = 8$?

   Ⓕ 6

   Ⓖ 7

   Ⓗ 60

   Ⓙ 45

3. If 24 students each bring 5 cans of food to school for the homeless, how many cans do they bring in all?

   Ⓐ $24 + 5 = c$

   Ⓑ $24 - 5 = c$

   Ⓒ $24 \times 5 = c$

   Ⓓ $24 \div 5 = c$

4. If $x + 9 = 27$, then $x =$

   Ⓕ 3

   Ⓖ 16

   Ⓗ 36

   Ⓙ 18

5. A carpenter has 10 pieces of wood that are each 8 feet long. She has to cut 2 feet from each piece of wood because of water damage. How much good wood does she have left?

   Ⓐ $(8 + 2) \times 10 = g$

   Ⓑ $(10 - 2) \times 8 = g$

   Ⓒ $(10 \times 8) - 2 = g$

   Ⓓ $(8 - 2) \times 10 = g$

6. An electrician has 300 feet of wire. He uses 275 feet and saves the rest for another job. How many feet of wire does he have left?

   Ⓕ $300 + f = 275$

   Ⓖ $300 + 275 = f$

   Ⓗ $300 - f = 275$

   Ⓙ $f = 300 + 275$

7. Evaluate $4a + 2b$, if $a = 2$ and $b = 3$.

   Ⓐ 14

   Ⓑ 8

   Ⓒ 6

   Ⓓ 2

8. Evaluate $2m - 3n$, if $m = 5$ and $n = 2$.

   Ⓕ 10

   Ⓖ 4

   Ⓗ 6

   Ⓙ 16

DIRECTIONS: For questions 9–12, use the following information. A bus driver began her route with an empty bus. She picked up 8 passengers at the first stop. Each passenger paid $1.50. At the next stop, 12 passengers got on. Half of them were senior citizens, so they paid only $0.75. At the third stop 5 more passengers got on the bus and 8 got off.

9. What was the total number of passengers that got on the bus?

   Ⓐ 17

   Ⓑ 25

   Ⓒ 19

   Ⓓ 33

GO

10. **What was the total amount of money the passengers paid?**

- (F) $37.50
- (G) $27.50
- (H) $33.00
- (J) $33.50

11. **After the third stop, how many people were on the bus?**

- (A) 33
- (B) 19
- (C) 18
- (D) 17

12. **At the fourth stop, 14 people got off and 3 got on. How many people were on the bus after the stop?**

- (F) 6
- (G) 28
- (H) 14
- (J) 22

DIRECTIONS: Choose the best answer.

13. $18 + 12 \times 3 \div 4$

- (A) 22.5
- (B) 25
- (C) 13.5
- (D) 27

14. **A ship is carrying 480 barrels of oil. Each barrel contains 200 liters of oil. How many kiloliters of oil is the ship carrying?**

- (F) 96,000 kL
- (G) 9,600 kL
- (H) 960 kL
- (J) 96 kL

15. $18 \div 2 \times 3$

- (A) 3
- (B) 24
- (C) 27
- (D) 25

16. $14 - 3 \times 2$

- (F) 8
- (G) 22
- (H) 9
- (J) 18

17. **The distance across a street is 15 yards 1 foot. What is this distance in feet?**

- (A) 45 feet
- (B) 16 feet
- (C) 46 feet
- (D) 6 feet

18. **Laura is 4 feet 11 inches tall. What is her height in inches?**

- (F) 15 inches
- (G) 59 inches
- (H) 48 inches
- (J) 58 inches

19. **Suppose you drank 5 liters of milk in a week. How many milliliters would that be?**

- (A) 5,000 milliliters
- (B) 500 milliliters
- (C) 50 milliliters
- (D) 5 milliliters

GO

20. 2 + 3 − 4

    (F)   1

    (G)   −1

    (H)   2

    (J)   −2

21. **There are 180 students and 6 classrooms. How many students will there be in each classroom?**

    (A)   40 students per classroom

    (B)   30 students per classroom

    (C)   20 students per classroom

    (D)   35 students per classroom

22. **A caterpillar crawls at 21 in./hr. to a vegetable patch. It took the caterpillar 20 minutes to get there. How far was the vegetable patch?**

    (F)   21 in.

    (G)   420 in.

    (H)   7 in.

    (J)   20 in.

23. **JoJo signed up for a magazine that cost him $60 for 12 months. What was his cost per month?**

    (A) $6 per month

    (B) $12 per month

    (C) $5.50 per month

    (D) $5 per month

24. **Sessa traveled 424 kilometers in 8 hours. What was her speed rate?**

    (F)   48 kilometers per hour

    (G)   53 kilometers per hour

    (H)   55 kilometers per hour

    (J)   63 kilometers per hour

25. **A test track is 1 mile around. A driver drives 1 lap at 160 mph. How long will it take to make 20 laps?**

    (A)   10 min.

    (B)   7.5 min.

    (C)   8 min.

    (D)   16 min.

26. **A person travels for 10 minutes at 10 mph and 20 minutes at 20 mph. How far did the person travel?**

    (F)   30 mi.

    (G) $1\frac{2}{3}$ mi.

    (H) $6\frac{2}{3}$ mi.

    (J) $8\frac{1}{3}$ mi.

27. **Alexander's car went 270 miles on 9 gallons of gas. What rate was he getting?**

    (A)   30 miles per gallon

    (B)   40 miles per gallon

    (C)   33 miles per gallon

    (D)   25 miles per gallon

28. **You travel 495 miles at 55 mph. How long does it take?**

    (F)   9 hours

    (G)   55 hours

    (H)   385 hours

    (J)   8 hours

GO

29. Find P = 2w + 2ℓ, if w = 9 inches and ℓ = 7 inches.

- (A) 64 in.
- (B) 16 in.
- (C) 32 in.
- (D) 25 in.

30. Find A = $\frac{1}{2}$ bh, if b = 17 meters and h = 10 meters.

- (F) 85 m^2
- (G) 170 m^2
- (H) 340 m^2
- (J) 42.5 m^2

31. Find A = ℓ × w, if ℓ = 33 feet and w = 22 feet.

- (A) 363 ft.^{2}
- (B) 110 ft.^{2}
- (C) 726 ft.^{2}
- (D) 220 ft.^{2}

32. Find C = pd, if d = 12 centimeters and p = 3.42 centimeters.

- (F) 37.68 cm^2
- (G) 41.04 cm^2
- (H) 3.508 cm^2
- (J) 452.16 cm^2

33. Evaluate 5g + 2h, if g = 1 and h = 4.

- (A) 13
- (B) 28
- (C) 22
- (D) 7

34. Find A = πr^2, if r = 23 millimeters.

- (F) 529 mm^2
- (G) 1661.06 mm^2
- (H) 72.22 mm^2
- (J) 144.44 mm^2

35. Find A = ℓ × w, if ℓ = 45 yards and w = 22 yards.

- (A) 67 yd.^{2}
- (B) 23 yd.^{2}
- (C) 2.05 yd.^{2}
- (D) 990 yd.^{2}

36. 8 + 56 ÷ 8

- (F) 8
- (G) 56
- (H) 15
- (J) 16

37. Name the figure.

- (A) $\overline{BC}$
- (B) $\overrightarrow{BC}$
- (C) $\overline{BC}$
- (D) $\overrightarrow{BC}$

B •————————————• C

38. Name the figure.

- (F) $\overline{AB}$
- (G) $\overrightarrow{AB}$
- (H) $\overline{AB}$
- (J) $\overleftrightarrow{AB}$

A ←———•————————•———→ B

39. Name the figure.

- (A) ∠R
- (B) ∠T
- (C) ∠STR
- (D) ∠RST

Name _____ Date _____

Algebra and Functions Test
Answer Sheet

1 (A) (B) (C) (D)   21 (A) (B) (C) (D)
2 (F) (G) (H) (J)   22 (F) (G) (H) (J)
3 (A) (B) (C) (D)   23 (A) (B) (C) (D)
4 (F) (G) (H) (J)   24 (F) (G) (H) (J)
5 (A) (B) (C) (D)   25 (A) (B) (C) (D)
6 (F) (G) (H) (J)   26 (F) (G) (H) (J)
7 (A) (B) (C) (D)   27 (A) (B) (C) (D)
8 (F) (G) (H) (J)   28 (F) (G) (H) (J)
9 (A) (B) (C) (D)   29 (A) (B) (C) (D)
10 (F) (G) (H) (J)   30 (F) (G) (H) (J)

11 (A) (B) (C) (D)   31 (A) (B) (C) (D)
12 (F) (G) (H) (J)   32 (F) (G) (H) (J)
13 (A) (B) (C) (D)   33 (A) (B) (C) (D)
14 (F) (G) (H) (J)   34 (F) (G) (H) (J)
15 (A) (B) (C) (D)   35 (A) (B) (C) (D)
16 (F) (G) (H) (J)   36 (F) (G) (H) (J)
17 (A) (B) (C) (D)   37 (A) (B) (C) (D)
18 (F) (G) (H) (J)   38 (F) (G) (H) (J)
19 (A) (B) (C) (D)   39 (A) (B) (C) (D)
20 (F) (G) (H) (J)

Measurement and Geometry Standards

1.0 Students deepen their understanding of the measurement of plane and solid shapes and use this understanding to solve problems:

1.1   Understand the concept of a constant such as p; know the formulas for the circumference and area of a circle. *(See page 125.)*

What it means:
- Students should know the formula for the circumference of a circle ($C = \pi d$) and the area of a circle ($A = \pi r^2$).

1.2   Know common estimates of p (3.14; $\frac{22}{7}$) and use these values to estimate and calculate the circumference and the area of circles; compare with actual measurements. *(See page 126.)*

1.3   Know and use the formulas for the volume of triangular prisms and cylinders (area of base x height); compare these formulas and explain the similarity between them and the formula for the volume of a rectangular solid. *(See page 127.)*

What it means:
- Students should know the volume formulas for a triangular prism ($\frac{1}{2}b \times h \times \ell$), a cylinder ($\pi r^2 \times \ell$), and a rectangular solid ($b \times h \times \ell$).

Name _____ Date _____

Math
1.1

Constants and Formulas

DIRECTIONS: Choose the best answer.

1. The formula for the circumference of a circle is _____.

   Ⓐ $C = \pi d$

   Ⓑ $A = \pi r^2$

   Ⓒ $C = \pi r^2$

   Ⓓ $A = \pi d$

2. The formula for the area of a circle is _____.

   Ⓕ $C = \pi d$

   Ⓖ $A = \pi r^2$

   Ⓗ $C = \pi r^2$

   Ⓙ $A = \pi d$

3. The circumference of a circle with a radius of 3 can be written as _____.

   Ⓐ $C = \pi(2 \times 3)$

   Ⓑ $A = \pi(3)^2$

   Ⓒ $C = \pi(3)^2$

   Ⓓ $A = \pi(2 \times 3)$

4. The area of a circle with a radius of 3 can be written as _____.

   Ⓕ $C = \pi(2 \times 3)$

   Ⓖ $A = \pi(3)^2$

   Ⓗ $C = \pi(3)^2$

   Ⓙ $A = \pi(2 \times 3)$

5. The circumference of a circle with a radius of 8 can be written as _____.

   Ⓐ $C = \pi(2 \times 8)$

   Ⓑ $A = \pi(8)^2$

   Ⓒ $C = \pi(8)^2$

   Ⓓ $A = \pi(2 \times 8)$

6. The area of a circle with a radius of 8 can be written as _____.

   Ⓕ $C = \pi(2 \times 8)$

   Ⓖ $A = \pi(8)^2$

   Ⓗ $C = \pi(8)^2$

   Ⓙ $A = \pi(2 \times 8)$

7. The circumference of a circle with a radius of 23 can be written as _____.

   Ⓐ $C = \pi(2 \times 23)$

   Ⓑ $A = \pi(23)^2$

   Ⓒ $C = \pi(23)^2$

   Ⓓ $A = \pi(2 \times 23)$

8. The area of a circle with a radius of 23 can be written as _____.

   Ⓕ $C = \pi(2 \times 23)$

   Ⓖ $A = \pi(23)^2$

   Ⓗ $C = \pi(23)^2$

   Ⓙ $A = \pi(2 \times 23)$

9. The circumference of a circle with a radius of 10 can be written as _____.

   Ⓐ $C = \pi(2 \times 10)$

   Ⓑ $A = \pi(10)^2$

   Ⓒ $C = \pi(10)^2$

   Ⓓ $A = \pi(2 \times 10)$

10. The area of a circle with a radius of 10 can be written as _____.

   Ⓕ $C = \pi(2 \times 10)$

   Ⓖ $A = \pi(2 \times 10)$

   Ⓗ $C = \pi(10)^2$

   Ⓙ $A = \pi(10)^2$

Name _____   Date _____

Circumference and Area

DIRECTIONS: Choose the best answer. Use $\pi = 3.14$.

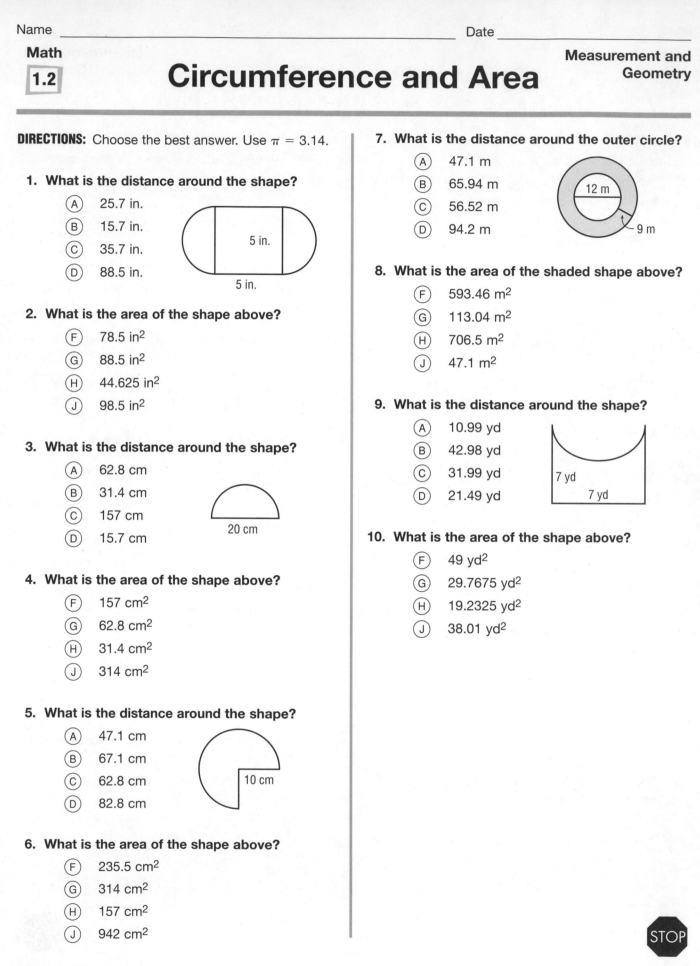

1. **What is the distance around the shape?**

   (A)   25.7 in.

   (B)   15.7 in.

   (C)   35.7 in.

   (D)   88.5 in.

   5 in.

   5 in.

2. **What is the area of the shape above?**

   (F)   78.5 in²

   (G)   88.5 in²

   (H)   44.625 in²

   (J)   98.5 in²

3. **What is the distance around the shape?**

   (A)   62.8 cm

   (B)   31.4 cm

   (C)   157 cm

   (D)   15.7 cm

   20 cm

4. **What is the area of the shape above?**

   (F)   157 cm²

   (G)   62.8 cm²

   (H)   31.4 cm²

   (J)   314 cm²

5. **What is the distance around the shape?**

   (A)   47.1 cm

   (B)   67.1 cm

   (C)   62.8 cm

   (D)   82.8 cm

   10 cm

6. **What is the area of the shape above?**

   (F)   235.5 cm²

   (G)   314 cm²

   (H)   157 cm²

   (J)   942 cm²

7. **What is the distance around the outer circle?**

   (A)   47.1 m

   (B)   65.94 m

   (C)   56.52 m

   (D)   94.2 m

   12 m

   9 m

8. **What is the area of the shaded shape above?**

   (F)   593.46 m²

   (G)   113.04 m²

   (H)   706.5 m²

   (J)   47.1 m²

9. **What is the distance around the shape?**

   (A)   10.99 yd

   (B)   42.98 yd

   (C)   31.99 yd

   (D)   21.49 yd

   7 yd

   7 yd

10. **What is the area of the shape above?**

   (F)   49 yd²

   (G)   29.7675 yd²

   (H)   19.2325 yd²

   (J)   38.01 yd²

STOP

Math

1.3

Measurement and Geometry

Volumes of Three-Dimensional Figures

DIRECTIONS: Choose the best answer.

1. Which of the following shapes is a triangular prism?

   (A)   (C)

   (B)   (D)

2. Which of the following shapes is a cylinder?

   (F)   (G)

   (H)   (J)

3. Which of the following shapes is a rectangular prism?

   (A)   (B)

   (C)   (D)

4. The formula for the volume of a triangular prism is _____.

   (F) $\ell \times w \times h$

   (G) $\frac{1}{2}b \times h$

   (H) $\frac{1}{2}b \times h \times \ell$

   (J) s^3

5. The formula for the volume of a cylinder is _____.

   (A) $\pi r^2 \times \ell$

   (B) $\pi d \times \ell$

   (C) $\pi b \times h \times \ell$

   (D) πr^2

6. The formula for the volume of a rectangular prism is _____.

   (F) $\ell \times w \times h$

   (G) $\frac{1}{2}b \times h$

   (H) $\frac{1}{2}b \times h \times \ell$

   (J) s^3

7. Find the volume of a triangular prism with base = 4 cm, height = 5 cm, and length = 8 cm.

   (A) 160 cm^3

   (B) 80 cm^3

   (C) 40 cm^3

   (D) 10 cm^3

8. Find the volume of a cylinder with radius = 5 and length = 7.

   (F) 109.9

   (G) 78.5

   (H) 175

   (J) 549.5

9. What is the volume of a rectangular prism with a length of 8 feet, a height of 6 feet, and a width of 2 feet?

   (A) 16 cubic feet

   (B) 18 cubic feet

   (C) 96 cubic feet

   (D) 32 cubic feet

STOP

Math

1.0

For pages 125–127

Mini-Test 1

DIRECTIONS: Choose the best answer.

1. The area of a circle with a radius of 5 can be written as _____.
   - (A) $\pi \times 2 \times 5$
   - (B) $\pi \times 5$
   - (C) $\pi \times 5^2$
   - (D) $\pi \times 2^2 \times 5$

2. The area of a circle with a radius of 12 can be written as _____.
   - (F) $\pi \times 12^2$
   - (G) $\pi \times 2^2 \times 12$
   - (H) $\pi \times 2 \times 12$
   - (J) $\pi \times 12$

3. The circumference of a circle with a radius of 12 can be written as _____.
   - (A) $\pi \times 12^2$
   - (B) $\pi \times 2^2 \times 12$
   - (C) $\pi \times 2 \times 12$
   - (D) $\pi \times 12$

4. What is the circumference of a circle with a radius of 10?
   - (F) $\pi \times 2 \times 10$
   - (G) $\pi \times 10$
   - (H) $\pi \times 2^2 \times 10$
   - (J) $\pi \times 10^2$

5. What is the area of a circle with a radius of 10?
   - (A) $\pi \times 2 \times 10$
   - (B) $\pi \times 10$
   - (C) $\pi \times 2^2 \times 10$
   - (D) $\pi \times 10^2$

6. What is the circumference of a circle with a diameter of 22?
   - (F) $\pi \times 22$
   - (G) $\pi \times 2 \times 22$
   - (H) $\pi \times 22^2$
   - (J) $\pi \times 2^2 \times 22$

7. Find the volume of a cylinder with a radius of 2 and a length of 9.
   - (A) 28.26
   - (B) 113.04
   - (C) 56.52
   - (D) 254.34

8. What is the volume of a rectangular prism with a length of 6 feet, a height of 4 feet, and a width of 3 feet?
   - (F) 36 cubic feet
   - (G) 288 cubic feet
   - (H) 72 cubic feet
   - (J) 216 cubic feet

9. Find the volume of a triangular prism with a base of 12 ft, height of 10 ft, and length of 6 ft.
   - (A) 720 ft^3
   - (B) 270 ft^3
   - (C) 180 ft^3
   - (D) 360 ft^3

STOP

Measurement and Geometry Standards

2.0 Students identify and describe the properties of two-dimensional figures:

2.1 Identify angles as vertical, adjacent, complementary, or supplementary and provide descriptions of these terms. *(See page 130.)*

What it means:
- Students should know definitions of types of angles: *vertical*– congruent angles on opposite sides of the same vertex; *adjacent*– angles that share a vertex and a common side between them; *complementary*– two angles whose sum is 90°; *supplementary*– two angles whose sum is 180°.

2.2 Use the properties of complementary and supplementary angles and the sum of the angles of a triangle to solve problems involving an unknown angle. *(See page 131.)*

2.3 Draw quadrilaterals and triangles from given information about them (e.g., a quadrilateral having equal sides but no right angles, a right isosceles triangle). *(See page 132.)*

What it means:
- Students should know that a quadrilateral is any four-sided shape.

Math

2.1

Identifying Angles

DIRECTIONS: Choose the best answer. Use the shape below for questions 1–4

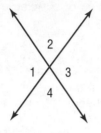

1. Angles 1 and 2 are _____.

- (A) vertical
- (B) adjacent

2. Angles 1 and 3 are _____.

- (F) vertical
- (G) adjacent

3. Angles 1 and 2 are _____.

- (A) complementary
- (B) supplementary
- (C) equal
- (D) none of the above

4. Angles 1 and 3 are _____.

- (F) complementary
- (G) supplementary
- (H) equal
- (J) none of the above

5. Supplementary means that the measure of two angles adds up to _____.

- (A) 45
- (B) 90
- (C) 180
- (D) 360

6. Complementary means that the measure of two angles adds up to _____.

- (F) 45
- (G) 90
- (H) 180
- (J) 360

7. Vertical angles are _____.

- (A) complementary
- (B) supplementary
- (C) equal
- (D) none of the above

8. Adjacent angles are _____.

- (F) complementary
- (G) supplementary
- (H) equal
- (J) none of the above

DIRECTIONS: Use the shape below for questions 9 and 10.

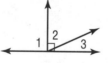

9. Angles 1 and 3 are _____.

- (A) complementary
- (B) supplementary
- (C) equal
- (D) none of the above

10. Angles 2 and 3 are _____.

- (F) complementary
- (G) supplementary
- (H) equal
- (J) none of the above

Name _____   Date _____

Finding the Measurement of Unknown Angles

Measurement and Geometry

DIRECTIONS: Choose the best answer.

1. If angles 1 and 2 are complementary and the measure of angle 1 is 46, what is the measure of angle 2?

   Ⓐ 34

   Ⓑ 44

   Ⓒ 134

   Ⓓ 314

2. If angles 3 and 4 are supplementary and the measure of angle 3 is 59, what is the measure of angle 4?

   Ⓕ 14

   Ⓖ 31

   Ⓗ 121

   Ⓙ 301

3. The sum of the measures of the three angles in a triangle is _____.

   Ⓐ 45

   Ⓑ 90

   Ⓒ 180

   Ⓓ 360

4. What is the missing measure in this triangle?

   Ⓕ 48

   Ⓖ 52

   Ⓗ 90

   Ⓙ 80

5. Two of the angles in a triangle measure 36 and 98. What is the measure of the third angle?

   Ⓐ 226

   Ⓑ 46

   Ⓒ 54

   Ⓓ 14

6. If angles 1 and 2 are complementary and the measure of angle 1 is 78, what is the measure of angle 2?

   Ⓕ 33

   Ⓖ 12

   Ⓗ 102

   Ⓙ 282

7. If angles 3 and 4 are supplementary and the measure of angle 3 is 78, what is the measure of angle 4?

   Ⓐ 33

   Ⓑ 12

   Ⓒ 102

   Ⓓ 282

DIRECTIONS: Use the shape below for questions 8 and 9.

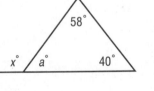

8. Find the measure of *a* in the triangle.

   Ⓕ 45

   Ⓖ 8

   Ⓗ 82

   Ⓙ 262

9. Find the measure of *x* in the figure.

   Ⓐ 98

   Ⓑ 82

   Ⓒ 8

   Ⓓ 38

STOP

Math
2.3

Drawing Quadrilaterals and Triangles

DIRECTIONS: Name and draw the described polygon.

1. Quadrilateral with all sides equal, opposite sides parallel, and four right angles.

2. Polygon with three equal sides.

3. Polygon with opposite sides equal and four right angles.

4. Polygon with three sides of different length.

5. Polygon with three sides, two of which are equal in length.

Math

2.0

Mini-Test 2

For pages 130–132

DIRECTIONS: Choose the best answer.

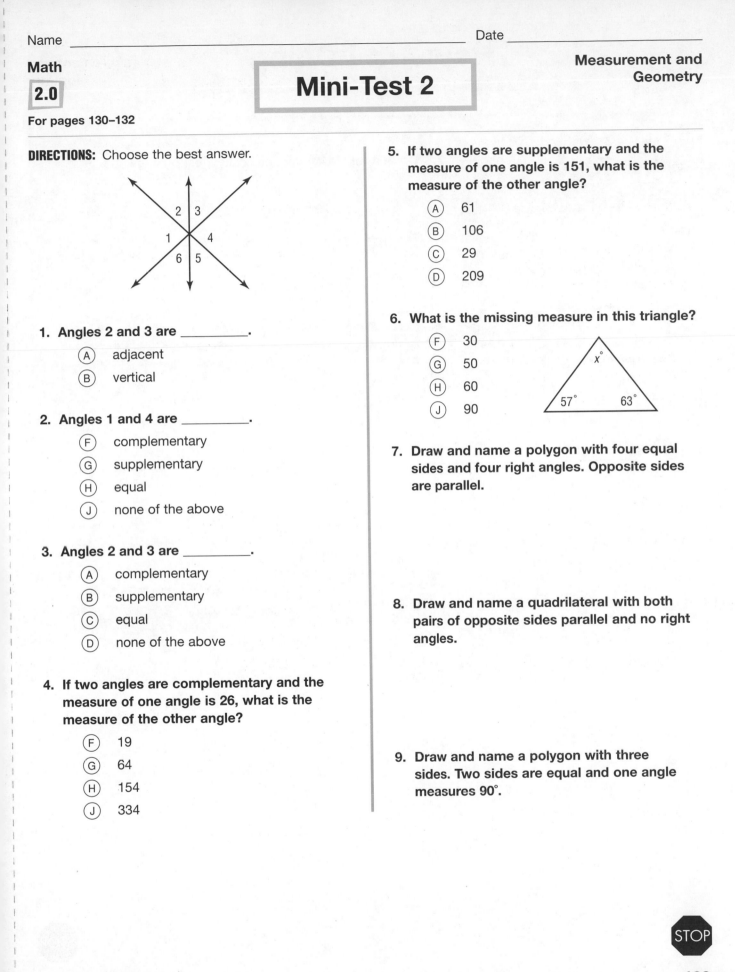

1. Angles 2 and 3 are _____.

   (A) adjacent

   (B) vertical

2. Angles 1 and 4 are _____.

   (F) complementary

   (G) supplementary

   (H) equal

   (J) none of the above

3. Angles 2 and 3 are _____.

   (A) complementary

   (B) supplementary

   (C) equal

   (D) none of the above

4. If two angles are complementary and the measure of one angle is 26, what is the measure of the other angle?

   (F) 19

   (G) 64

   (H) 154

   (J) 334

5. If two angles are supplementary and the measure of one angle is 151, what is the measure of the other angle?

   (A) 61

   (B) 106

   (C) 29

   (D) 209

6. What is the missing measure in this triangle?

   (F) 30

   (G) 50

   (H) 60

   (J) 90

7. Draw and name a polygon with four equal sides and four right angles. Opposite sides are parallel.

8. Draw and name a quadrilateral with both pairs of opposite sides parallel and no right angles.

9. Draw and name a polygon with three sides. Two sides are equal and one angle measures 90°.

STOP

How Am I Doing?

Mini-Test 1 Page 128 **Number Correct**	**7** answers correct	**Great Job!** Move on to the section test on page 135.
	5–6 answers correct	**You're almost there!** But you still need a little practice. Review practice pages 125–127 before moving on to the section test on page 135.
	0–4 answers correct	**Oops!** Time to review what you have learned and try again. Review the practice section on pages 125–127. Then retake the test on page 128. Now move on to the section test on page 135.
Mini-Test 2 Page 133 **Number Correct**	**8–9** answers correct	**Awesome!** Move on to the section test on page 135.
	5–7 answers correct	**You're almost there!** But you still need a little practice. Review practice pages 130–132 before moving on to the section test on page 135.
	0–4 answers correct	**Oops!** Time to review what you have learned and try again. Review the practice section on pages 130–132. Then retake the test on page 133. Now move on to the section test on page 135.

Name _____   Date _____

Final Measurement and Geometry Test
for pages 125–133

DIRECTIONS: Choose the best answer. Use $\pi = 3.14$.

1. The area of a circle with a radius of 15 can be written as _____.

   (A) $\pi \times 15^2$

   (B) $\pi \times 2 \times 15$

   (C) $\pi \times 2^2 \times 15$

   (D) $\pi \times 15$

2. The area of a circle with a diameter of 4 can be written as _____.

   (F) $\pi \times 4$

   (G) $\pi \times 2 \times 4$

   (H) $\pi \times (\frac{1}{2} \times 4)^2$

   (J) $\pi \times 4^2$

3. The circumference of a circle with a diameter of 4 can be written as _____.

   (A) $\pi \times 4$

   (B) $\pi \times 2 \times 4$

   (C) $\pi \times (\frac{1}{2} \times 4)^2$

   (D) $\pi \times 4^2$

4. The area of a circle with a radius of 18 can be written as _____.

   (F) $\pi \times 18$

   (G) $\pi \times 2 \times 18$

   (H) $\pi \times 18^2$

   (J) $\pi \times 2^2 \times 18$

5. The circumference of a circle with a radius of 18 can be written as _____.

   (A) $\pi \times 18$

   (B) $\pi \times 2 \times 18$

   (C) $\pi \times 18^2$

   (D) $\pi \times 2^2 \times 18$

6. What is the circumference of a circle with a radius of 7?

   (F) 43.96

   (G) 21.98

   (H) 153.86

   (J) 87.92

7. What is the area of a circle with a radius of 7?

   (A) 43.96

   (B) 21.98

   (C) 153.86

   (D) 87.92

8. What is the area of a circle with a diameter of 22?

   (F) 69.08

   (G) 138.16

   (H) 1519.76

   (J) 379.94

9. What is the area of a circle with a radius of 2?

   (A) 50.24

   (B) 6.28

   (C) 12.56

   (D) 25.12

10. What is the circumference of a circle with a diameter of 4?

   (F) 50.24

   (G) 6.28

   (H) 12.56

   (J) 25.12

GO

11. Find the volume of a cylinder with radius = 3 and length = 15.

  (A) 282.6

  (B) 423.9

  (C) 141.3

  (D) 211.95

12. Find the volume of a triangular prism with base = 8 m, height = 3 m, and length = 11 m.

  (F) 66 m^3

  (G) 264 m^3

  (H) 528 m^3

  (J) 132 m^3

13. Find the volume of a cylinder with radius = 9 and length = 2.

  (A) 508.68

  (B) 254.34

  (C) 56.52

  (D) 113.04

14. What is the volume of a rectangular prism with a length of 4 feet, a height of 2 feet, and a width of 1 foot?

  (F) 16 cubic feet

  (G) 12 cubic feet

  (H) 8 cubic feet

  (J) 4 cubic feet

15. Find the volume of a triangular prism with base = 7 yd., height = 7 yd., and length = 8 yd.

  (A) 392 cubic yards

  (B) 98 cubic yards

  (C) 784 cubic yards

  (D) 196 cubic yards

16. Find the volume of a triangular prism with base = 6 yd., height = 3 yd., and length = 10 yd.

  (F) 180 yd.^{2}

  (G) 10 yd.^{3}

  (H) 39 yd.^{3}

  (J) 90 yd.^{3}

DIRECTIONS: Use the figure below for questions 17–21.

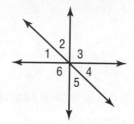

17. Angles 1 and 4 are _____.

  (A) adjacent

  (B) vertical

18. Angles 1 and 2 are _____.

  (F) adjacent

  (G) vertical

19. Angles 1 and 4 are _____.

  (A) complementary

  (B) supplementary

  (C) equal

  (D) none of the above

20. Angles 1 and 2 are _____.

  (F) complementary

  (G) supplementary

  (H) equal

  (J) none of the above

21. Angles 3 and 6 are _____.

  (A) adjacent

  (B) vertical

22. If angles 1 and 2 are complementary and the measure of angle 1 is 35, what is the measure of angle 2?

  (F) 10

  (G) 55

  (H) 145

  (J) 325

GO

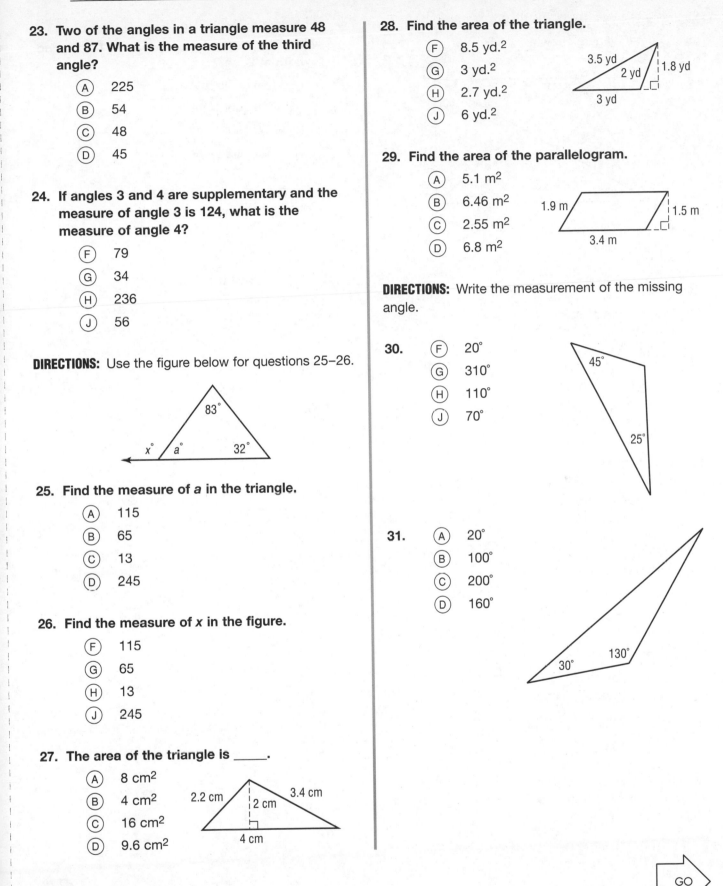

23. Two of the angles in a triangle measure 48 and 87. What is the measure of the third angle?

   (A) 225

   (B) 54

   (C) 48

   (D) 45

24. If angles 3 and 4 are supplementary and the measure of angle 3 is 124, what is the measure of angle 4?

   (F) 79

   (G) 34

   (H) 236

   (J) 56

DIRECTIONS: Use the figure below for questions 25–26.

25. Find the measure of *a* in the triangle.

   (A) 115

   (B) 65

   (C) 13

   (D) 245

26. Find the measure of *x* in the figure.

   (F) 115

   (G) 65

   (H) 13

   (J) 245

27. The area of the triangle is _____.

   (A) 8 cm^2

   (B) 4 cm^2

   (C) 16 cm^2

   (D) 9.6 cm^2

28. Find the area of the triangle.

   (F) 8.5 yd.^{2}

   (G) 3 yd.^{2}

   (H) 2.7 yd.^{2}

   (J) 6 yd.^{2}

29. Find the area of the parallelogram.

   (A) 5.1 m^2

   (B) 6.46 m^2

   (C) 2.55 m^2

   (D) 6.8 m^2

DIRECTIONS: Write the measurement of the missing angle.

30.   (F) 20°

      (G) 310°

      (H) 110°

      (J) 70°

31.   (A) 20°

      (B) 100°

      (C) 200°

      (D) 160°

GO

DIRECTIONS: Choose the measurement of the angles given from the figure shown.

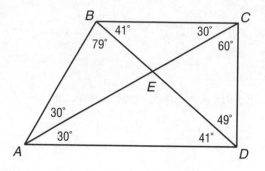

32. ∠BEA

    (F)   238°

    (G)   71°

    (H)   119°

    (J)   49°

33. ∠AED

    (A)   71°

    (B)   11°

    (C)   109°

    (D)   110°

34. ∠DEC

    (F)   109°

    (G)   71°

    (H)   142°

    (J)   91°

35. ∠CEB

    (A)   129°

    (B)   149°

    (C)   71°

    (D)   109°

36. What is the volume of a rectangular prism with a length of 8 feet, a height of 6 feet, and a width of 2 feet?

    (F)   16 cubic feet

    (G)   18 cubic feet

    (H)   96 cubic feet

    (J)   32 cubic feet

37. What is the volume of a cylinder with a radius of 3 ft and length of 10 ft?

    (A)   36 ft.^{3}

    (B)   282.6 ft.^{3}

    (C)   113.04 ft.^{2}

    (D)   30 ft.^{2}

Name _____   Date _____

Measurement and Geometry Test
Answer Sheet

1 (A) (B) (C) (D)	21 (A) (B) (C) (D)
2 (F) (G) (H) (J)	22 (F) (G) (H) (J)
3 (A) (B) (C) (D)	23 (A) (B) (C) (D)
4 (F) (G) (H) (J)	24 (F) (G) (H) (J)
5 (A) (B) (C) (D)	25 (A) (B) (C) (D)
6 (F) (G) (H) (J)	26 (F) (G) (H) (J)
7 (A) (B) (C) (D)	27 (A) (B) (C) (D)
8 (F) (G) (H) (J)	28 (F) (G) (H) (J)
9 (A) (B) (C) (D)	29 (A) (B) (C) (D)
10 (F) (G) (H) (J)	30 (F) (G) (H) (J)
11 (A) (B) (C) (D)	31 (A) (B) (C) (D)
12 (F) (G) (H) (J)	32 (F) (G) (H) (J)
13 (A) (B) (C) (D)	33 (A) (B) (C) (D)
14 (F) (G) (H) (J)	34 (F) (G) (H) (J)
15 (A) (B) (C) (D)	35 (A) (B) (C) (D)
16 (F) (G) (H) (J)	36 (F) (G) (H) (J)
17 (A) (B) (C) (D)	37 (A) (B) (C) (D)
18 (F) (G) (H) (J)	
19 (A) (B) (C) (D)	
20 (F) (G) (H) (J)	

Statistics, Data Analysis and Probability Standards

1.0 Students compute and analyze statistical measurements for data sets:

1.1 Compute the range, mean, median, and mode of data sets. *(See page 141.)*

What it means:
- Students should know that the mode of a set of data is the one that occurs most often.
- Students should know that the median of a set of data is the number in the middle when the numbers are put in order.

1.2 Understand how additional data added to data sets may affect these computations of measures of central tendency. *(See page 142.)*

1.3 Understand how the inclusion or exclusion of outliers affects measures of central tendency. *(See page 143.)*

What it means:
- Students should know that an outlier for a set of data is any value that is markedly smaller or larger than other values.

1.4 Know why a specific measure of central tendency (mean, median, mode) provides the most useful information in a given context. *(See page 144.)*

Name _____   Date _____

Math
1.1

Range, Mean, Median, and Mode

DIRECTIONS: Use this data set for the example and questions 1–4.

The average number of rainy days per month in Sun City, Florida, are: 8, 5, 8, 8, 10, 13, 17, 17, 25, 20, 7, 9.

1. **What is the range of the data?**
   - (A) 8
   - (B) 9.5
   - (C) 12.25
   - (D) 20

2. **What is the mean of the data?**
   - (F) 8
   - (G) 9.5
   - (H) 12.25
   - (J) 20

3. **What is the median of the data?**
   - (A) 8
   - (B) 9.5
   - (C) 12.25
   - (D) 20

4. **What is the mode of the data?**
   - (F) 8
   - (G) 9.5
   - (H) 12.25
   - (J) 20

DIRECTIONS: Use this data set for questions 5–7.

The average basketball attendance per game for the season was: 80, 100, 60, 120, 120, 100, 140.

5. **What is the range of the data?**
   - (A) 80
   - (B) 100
   - (C) 100, 120
   - (D) 102.9

6. **What is the mean of the data?**
   - (F) 80
   - (G) 100
   - (H) 100, 120
   - (J) 102.9

7. **What is the median of the data?**
   - (A) 80
   - (B) 100
   - (C) 100, 120
   - (D) 102.9

Math

1.2

Analyzing Data Sets

DIRECTIONS: Cora's quiz scores one week were 10, 8, 9, 10, 8, 8, 9.

1. **What is the mean of the scores?**
   - (A)   8.86
   - (B)   8
   - (C)   8.88
   - (D)   9

2. **What is the mean if Cora gets a 2 on the 8th quiz?**
   - (F)   8.86
   - (G)   8
   - (H)   8.88
   - (J)   9

3. **What is the mean if Cora gets a 9 on the 8th quiz?**
   - (A)   8.86
   - (B)   8
   - (C)   8.88
   - (D)   9

4. **What is the mean if Cora gets a 10 on the 8th quiz?**
   - (F)   8.86
   - (G)   8
   - (H)   8.88
   - (J)   9

5. **What is the median of the scores?**
   - (A)   10
   - (B)   9
   - (C)   8.5
   - (D)   8

6. **What is the median if Cora gets a 2 on the 8th quiz?**
   - (F)   8
   - (G)   8.5
   - (H)   9
   - (J)   10

7. **What is the median if Cora gets a 9 on the 8th quiz?**
   - (A)   10
   - (B)   9
   - (C)   8.5
   - (D)   8

8. **What is the median if Cora gets a 10 on the 8th quiz?**
   - (F)   8
   - (G)   8.5
   - (H)   9
   - (J)   10

9. **What is the mode if Cora gets a 9 on the 8th quiz?**
   - (A)   8
   - (B)   8, 9
   - (C)   9
   - (D)   10

STOP

Math

1.3

Outliers

DIRECTIONS: Use this data set for all the questions. Tanya's scores on a series of tests were: 83, 83, 74, 74, 74, 87, 82, 73, 76, 84, 94, 88.

Example:

What would the range of the data be if the two lowest scores were dropped?

(A) 22

(B) 21

(C) 20

(D) 18

Answer: (D)

1. What would the median be if the two lowest scores were dropped?

(A) 82

(B) 82.5

(C) 83

(D) 83.5

2. What is the mean? Use the scores.

(F) 81

(G) 82.5

(H) 81.5

(J) 82

3. What would the mode be if the two lowest scores were dropped?

(A) 74, 83

(B) 74

(C) 83

(D) 82

4. What would the median be if Tanya got 100 on her next test? Use all the scores.

(F) 82

(G) 82.5

(H) 83.5

(J) 83

5. What would the mode be if Tanya got 100 on her next test? Use all the scores.

(A) 74, 83

(B) 74

(C) 83

(D) 100

6. What would the range of the data be if Tanya got 100 on her next test? Use all the scores.

(F) 20

(G) 21

(H) 26

(J) 27

STOP

Statistics, Data Analysis, and Probability

Using Means, Medians, and Modes

DIRECTIONS: A used car lot has the following vehicles for sale. Use the chart for questions 1–4 to determine which measure of central tendency would best show the information requested.

Vehicle	Camaro	Civic	Escort	Ranger	Storm	Daytona
Doors	2	4	2	4	4	4
Miles	23,000	31,000	120,000	33,000	20,000	35,000
Color	black	blue	red	white	blue	blue
Color	$8,995	$7,999	$5,995	$7,995	$8,995	$6,995

1. **number of doors**
   - (A) mean
   - (B) median
   - (C) mode
   - (D) none of the above

2. **number of miles**
   - (F) mean
   - (G) median
   - (H) mode
   - (J) none of the above

3. **color**
   - (A) mean
   - (B) median
   - (C) mode
   - (D) none of the above

4. **price**
   - (F) mean
   - (G) median
   - (H) mode
   - (J) none of the above

DIRECTIONS: Choose the best answer.

5. **The mode best describes a set of data when _____.**
   - (A) it is desired to know the most frequent item or number
   - (B) there are no numbers that differ greatly from the rest
   - (C) there are numbers that are much greater or less than the majority of the numbers
   - (D) there are more than five numbers

6. **The median best describes a set of data when _____.**
   - (F) it is desired to know the most frequent item or number
   - (G) there are no numbers that differ greatly from the rest
   - (H) there are numbers that are much greater or less than the majority of the numbers
   - (J) there are more than five numbers

Name _____   Date _____

Math

Statistics, Data Analysis,
and Probability

For pages 141–144

DIRECTIONS: Use the data set for the questions 1–4. The test scores for a class are: 86, 94, 70, 81, 92, 74, 75, 89, 76, 97.

1. **What is the mean of the data?**

   (A) 27

   (B) 83.4

   (C) 83.5

   (D) none

2. **What is the median of the data?**

   (F) 27

   (G) 83.4

   (H) 83.5

   (J) none

3. **If five more scores are added (72, 75, 83, 76, 88), what is the mean of the data?**

   (A) 83.4

   (B) 83.5

   (C) 81.9

   (D) 81

4. **If five more scores are added (72, 75, 83, 76, 88), what is the median of the data?**

   (F) 83.4

   (G) 83.5

   (H) 81.9

   (J) 81

5. **If the set of scores now includes a 0 for a student that didn't make up the test, what is the mean for the scores?**

   (A) 81.9

   (B) 75.8

   (C) 83.4

   (D) 84.9

6. **If the student did make up the test and earned a 100, what is the mean for the scores?**

   (F) 81.9

   (G) 75.8

   (H) 83.4

   (J) 84.9

7. **The quiz grades in a Spanish class are shown in the table. The mode is 35, the median is 33, and the mean is 30.8. Which measure best represents the data?**

Grades	35	33	32	15
Frequency	5	4	2	2

   (A) mean

   (B) median

   (C) mode

   (D) none of the above

8. **The English test scores for a class are shown in the table. The mean is 89.8, the mode is 86, and the median is 88.5. Which measure best represents the data?**

Scores	100	96	92	88	84	80
Frequency	2	3	5	7	3	1

   (F) mean

   (G) median

   (H) mode

   (J) none of the above

STOP

Statistics, Data Analysis and Probability Standards

2.0 Students use data samples of a population and describe the characteristics and limitations of the samples:

2.1 Compare different samples of a population with the data from the entire population and identify a situation in which it makes sense to use a sample. *(See page 147.)*

2.2 Identify different ways of selecting a sample (e.g., convenience sampling, responses to a survey, random sampling) and which method makes a sample more representative for a population. *(See page 148.)*

2.3 Analyze data displays and explain why the way in which the question was asked might have influenced the results obtained and why the way in which the results were displayed might have influenced the conclusions reached. *(See page 149.)*

2.4 Identify data that represent sampling errors and explain why the sample (and the display) might be biased. *(See page 150.)*

2.5 Identify claims based on statistical data and, in simple cases, evaluate the validity of the claims. *(See page 151.)*

Math

2.1

Using Samples

 Clue   Read each problem carefully and make sure you understand what is being asked.

DIRECTIONS: Explain your answers in complete sentences.

1. In a random sample of 35 students in the school cafeteria, Marsha found that 15 ordered spaghetti. If there are 525 students who eat the cafeteria lunch, how many will likely order spaghetti?

_____

_____

_____

2. Is the sample in question 1 a good sampling of the population? Explain.

_____

_____

_____

3. Why might you choose to use the sample survey rather than survey the entire population? Explain.

_____

_____

_____

4. Mickey took a survey of sweatshirt sizes from a random sample of 25 students. The shirts are to be sold in a bookstore at a school with 950 students. Should the sample be larger? Explain.

_____

_____

5. A pre-election poll predicted that a certain candidate for the school board would receive 30% of the vote. She actually received 10,921 votes. Estimate how many people voted in the election.

_____

_____

_____

6. A pre-election poll predicted that a certain candidate for county treasurer would receive 25% of the vote. He actually received 75%. Was this poll useful? Explain.

_____

_____

_____

7. Give two reasons why the pre-election poll could have been so far off in question 6.

_____

_____

_____

Selecting Appropriate Samples

DIRECTIONS: Explain your answer in complete sentences.

1. If a survey is taken of students at a basketball camp, would the results be biased if the questions concern favorite sports? Explain.

_____

_____

_____

2. Would the students at a basketball camp be a good sample population to represent a school's student population? Explain.

_____

_____

_____

3. The entire sixth grade filled out a survey. Would this be a good sample population for a survey on favorite music of sixth graders? Explain.

_____

_____

_____

4. Zoo visitors are asked their opinion on poaching. Is this a good sample population? Explain.

_____

_____

5. Bookstore visitors are asked their opinion on poaching. Is this a good sample population? Explain.

_____

_____

_____

6. Is surveying people at the mall an example of convenience sampling? Explain.

_____

_____

_____

7. Waiters at a steak restaurant are asked their opinion of specialty diets, such as vegetarianism. Is this a random sampling? Explain.

_____

_____

_____

8. Visitors to the White House are asked their opinion on the national budget for art development. Is this a random sampling? Explain.

_____

_____

Name _____   Date _____

DIRECTIONS: The monthly rainfall recorded, in centimeters, at Mountain Valley Resort last year was as follows.

J	F	M	A	M	J	J	A	S	O	N	D
0	2	7	12	18	24	25	25	22	6	3	0

Here is part of the resort's brochure: Beautiful Summer Weather: Average monthly rainfall less than 10 centimeters!

1. **Which measure of central tendency was used in the brochure?**

    (A) mean

    (B) median

    (C) mode

    (D) range

2. **Which measure of central tendency would be a better indicator of rainfall during the summer?**

    (F) mean

    (G) median

    (H) mode

    (J) range

3. **Why is the brochure misleading?**

    (A) It doesn't mention the cabins.

    (B) The average monthly rainfall is much less than 10 centimeters.

    (C) The average monthly rainfall is much more than 10 centimeters.

    (D) It doesn't mention the price.

DIRECTIONS: Choose the best answer.

4. **Furniture World has seven salespeople. The commissions they earned last week were $493, $289, $305, $299, $366, $308, and $299. The owner of the store places an ad in the newspaper for additional salespeople. The want ad states: Experienced Salespeople wanted for furniture store. Earn an average weekly commission of $335. Which measure of central tendency is used in the ad?**

    (F) mean

    (G) median

    (H) mode

    (J) range

5. **Which measure(s) of central tendency would be useful to a person considering a sales position at Furniture World?**

    (A) mean

    (B) median

    (C) median and mode

    (D) mean and mode

6. **How many of the salespeople make the advertised amount or higher?**

    (F) 6

    (G) 4

    (H) 2

    (J) 1

Identifying Sampling Errors and Bias

DIRECTIONS: Answers questions 1-6 in complete sentences.

A concert organizer wants to identify what type of music is most popular with adults in a Midwestern city. The organizer has considered using various sampling methods. Explain why each of the following should or should not be used.

1. **Ask the first 30 adults who arrive for a concert at Symphony Hall.**

   _____

   _____

   _____

2. **Ask all adults who shop in music stores located in an area of the city elected at random.**

   _____

   _____

   _____

3. **Ask all adults living in the city whose phone numbers end with the digit 3.**

   _____

   _____

   _____

A cereal manufacturer wants to identify the most popular type of breakfast food. The manufacturer decides to include a questionnaire in every tenth box of cereal that it packages.

4. **Is this a good example of random sampling? Explain.**

   _____

   _____

   _____

5. **Are the results of this survey likely to be biased? Explain.**

   _____

   _____

   _____

6. **Nina wants to know the most popular book of sixth graders. She asks 20 sixth grade boys out of the 200 sixth graders in her school. Is this a good survey method? Explain.**

   _____

   _____

   _____

DIRECTIONS: Choose the best answer.

7. **The field trip committee wants to survey students so the sample represents all of the students. Which of the following could be used?**

   Ⓐ Survey one student from each lunch table.

   Ⓑ Survey every eighth student on the current roster.

   Ⓒ Survey every fifteenth student leaving the building one afternoon.

   Ⓓ Any of the above.

Name _____   Date _____

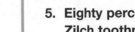

DIRECTIONS: Answer the questions in complete sentences.

A television commercial makes the following claim:

"In a national taste-test, 7 out of 10 teenagers preferred our brand of cola to our competitor's."

1. **What is meant by "a national taste-test"? Explain.**

   _____

   _____

2. **Interpret the statistic "7 out of 10 teenagers."**

   _____

   _____

   _____

3. **How is this advertiser trying to influence consumers?**

   _____

   _____

   _____

4. **Is it possible that this statistic is not truly representative of the nation's preference? Explain.**

   _____

   _____

   _____

Tell why each of the following advertisements is misleading.

5. **Eighty percent of all dentists surveyed agree: Zilch toothpaste tastes best.**

   _____

   _____

   _____

6. **In the past 5 years, 25,000 cola drinkers have switched to Koala Kola.**

   _____

   _____

   _____

7. **Thousands of teenagers wake in the morning to a glass of Zest. It has 20% real fruit juice and 100% bounce.**

   _____

   _____

   _____

8. **The best athletes choose Great Fit Shoes.**

   _____

   _____

   _____

Math

2.0

For pages 147–157

Mini-Test 2

Statistics, Data Analysis,
and Probability

DIRECTIONS: Answer each question in complete sentences.

1. A store advertises that more people buy brand A toothpaste than any other. With a little research, you find that the survey was done by age group and the store is only using the age group of children under six. The results from the rest of the survey were supportive of brand B. Was this a good sample? Explain.

_____

_____

_____

2. Phone surveys are frequently done before elections. In order to be a good sampling of the general population, how should the phone number selection be done? Explain.

_____

_____

_____

3. Would asking individuals as they enter the mall be a good means of getting a random sampling for a survey on popular TV shows? Explain.

_____

_____

_____

4. To identify the time most parents set as a curfew on Friday nights, all students attending the 9:00 P.M. show at one movie theater were surveyed. Are the results of this survey likely to be biased? Explain.

_____

_____

5. Suppose you want to find out the favorite sport among teenagers in your town. If you surveyed every eighth teenager who enters a stadium for one particular game would you be getting an unbiased result? Explain.

_____

_____

_____

6. A television ad says, "More than 100 dentists can't be wrong. XYZ toothpaste is the one you should use for a healthier smile." Tell why this advertisement might be misleading.

_____

_____

_____

DIRECTIONS: Tell whether mean, median, or mode is best to use when describing the following.

7. 48, 48, 47, 46, 43

(A) mean

(B) median

(C) mode

8. Populations of California, Nevada, Wyoming, Idaho, Utah

(F) mean

(G) median

(H) mode

9. 10, 320, 300, 295

(A) mean

(B) median

(C) mode

Statistics, Data Analysis, and Probability Standards

3.0 Students determine theoretical and experimental probabilities and use these to make predictions about events:

3.1 Represent all possible outcomes for compound events in an organized way (e.g., tables, grids, tree diagrams) and express the theoretical probability of each outcome. *(See page 154.)*

3.2 Use data to estimate the probability of future events (e.g., batting averages or number of accidents per mile driven). *(See page 155.)*

3.3 Represent probabilities as ratios, proportions, decimals between 0 and 1, and percentages between 0 and 100 and verify that the probabilities computed are reasonable; know that if P is the probability of an event, 1-*P* is the probability of an event not occurring. *(See page 156.)*

3.4 Understand that the probability of either of two disjoint events occurring is the sum of the two individual probabilities and that the probability of one event following another, in independent trials, is the product of the two probabilities. *(See page 157.)*

3.5 Understand the difference between independent and dependent events. *(See page 158.)*

Probability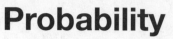

 Clue Choose "not given" only if you are sure the right answer is not one of the choices. Look for key words, numbers, and figures in each problem, and be sure you perform the correct operation.

DIRECTIONS: Choose the best answer

1. There are 10 silver earrings and 10 gold earrings in a drawer. Cheryl reaches into her jewelry box without looking. What is the probability that she will pick a gold earring?

   (A) $\frac{1}{2}$

   (B) $\frac{1}{3}$

   (C) $\frac{1}{4}$

   (D) not given

2. A group of teachers are ordering sandwiches from the deli. They can choose ham, beef, turkey, or bologna on white bread, wheat bread, or rye bread. How many different meat and bread combinations are possible?

   (F) 12

   (G) 16

   (H) 7

   (J) not given

3. Elliott spun the arrow on a spinner 30 times. The results are shown in the table. Which of these spinners did Elliott most likely spin?

Diamond	Heart	Spade	Total Spins
11	10	9	30

   (A)   (B)   (C)   (D)

4. A snack food company makes chewy fruit shapes of lions, monkeys, elephants, and giraffes, in red, green, purple, and yellow. They put the same number of each kind in a package. How many different outcomes are there?

   (F) 4

   (G) 8

   (H) 16

   (J) not given

DIRECTIONS: For questions 5 and 6, draw a tree diagram to show all the outcomes.

5. Draw the diagram for question 1.

6. A new car can be ordered in black, red, or tan. You may also choose leather or fabric seats. Show the outcomes.

 STOP

Math
3.2

Future Probability

DIRECTIONS: Use the following data for questions 1–4.

About 7% of all Ohio drivers are teens. Teens have 17% of all Ohio crashes. About 5% of U.S. drivers are teens. Teens have 15% of all U.S. crashes.

1. **Out of 100 cars in a parking lot in Ohio, how many would you expect to be driven by teens?**

   Ⓐ 7
   Ⓑ 5
   Ⓒ 15
   Ⓓ 17

2. **Out of 100 cars in a parking lot in California, how many would you expect to be driven by teens?**

   Ⓕ 7
   Ⓖ 5
   Ⓗ 15
   Ⓙ 17

3. **If there were 200 accidents in Ohio in one month, how many would you expect to involve a teen?**

   Ⓐ 14
   Ⓑ 10
   Ⓒ 30
   Ⓓ 34

4. **If there were 200 accidents in Utah in one month, how many would you expect to involve a teen?**

   Ⓕ 14
   Ⓖ 10
   Ⓗ 30
   Ⓙ 34

DIRECTIONS: Choose the best answer.

The following are 2002 batting averages for five Cincinnati Reds. Kearns, .315; Walker, .299; Larson, .275; Griffey .264; Casey .261.

5. **How many hits would you expect Kearns to make out of the next 10 games?**

   Ⓐ 315
   Ⓑ 31
   Ⓒ 3
   Ⓓ .3

6. **How many hits would you expect Larson to make out of the next 20 games?**

   Ⓕ 275
   Ⓖ 2.75
   Ⓗ 3
   Ⓙ 5

7. **What is Griffey's batting average written as hits out of 100 attempts?**

   Ⓐ .264
   Ⓑ 26.4
   Ⓒ 264
   Ⓓ 2.64

8. **In 10 games, what would be the difference in hits between Kearns and Casey?**

   Ⓕ 3
   Ⓖ 2
   Ⓗ 1
   Ⓙ 0

Name _____   Date _____

Probability

DIRECTIONS: Choose the best answer.

For questions 1–4, suppose you wrote the word VACATION on a strip of paper and cut the paper into pieces with one letter per piece. If you put the pieces into a hat and pulled out one piece without looking, determine the probability of each situation.

1. **What is the probability that you would pick out the letter A?**
    - Ⓐ 1 out of 8
    - Ⓑ 2 out of 8
    - Ⓒ 4 out of 5
    - Ⓓ 2 out of 7

2. **Without returning the A to the hat, what is the probability that you would pick out the letter C?**
    - Ⓕ 1 out of 8
    - Ⓖ 1 out of 7
    - Ⓗ 2 out of 8
    - Ⓙ 1 out of 6

3. **Without returning the A or the C to the hat, what is the probability of picking a vowel?**
    - Ⓐ 4 out of 8
    - Ⓑ 3 out of 7
    - Ⓒ 3 out of 5
    - Ⓓ 3 out of 6

4. **Given the original word, what is the probability of picking a consonant?**
    - Ⓕ 1 out of 8
    - Ⓖ 4 out of 8
    - Ⓗ 2 out of 8
    - Ⓙ 4 out of 6

There are ten white tennis balls and ten green tennis balls in a box. Tony reaches into the box without looking.

5. **What is the probability that he will pick a white ball?**

    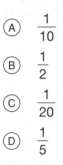
    - Ⓐ $\frac{1}{10}$
    - Ⓑ $\frac{1}{2}$
    - Ⓒ $\frac{1}{20}$
    - Ⓓ $\frac{1}{5}$

6. **What is the probability that he will pick a green ball?**

    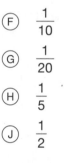
    - Ⓕ $\frac{1}{10}$
    - Ⓖ $\frac{1}{20}$
    - Ⓗ $\frac{1}{5}$
    - Ⓙ $\frac{1}{2}$

7. **Tony picks a white ball. He returns it to the box. He wants another white ball. What is the probability that he will pick a white ball from the box on the next try?**

    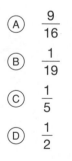
    - Ⓐ $\frac{9}{16}$
    - Ⓑ $\frac{1}{19}$
    - Ⓒ $\frac{1}{5}$
    - Ⓓ $\frac{1}{2}$

Math
3.4

Probability

Example:

A box contains 24 cards. Each card has a whole number written on it ranging from 2 to 25. If a card is picked at random from the box, returned, and a new card is picked, what is the probability one of the cards will be a prime number?

(A) $\frac{9}{24}$

(B) $\frac{18}{48}$

(C) $\frac{9}{13}$

(D) $\frac{3}{4}$

Answer: (D)

DIRECTIONS: Choose the best answer.

1. 50 people work in Raynel's office and 75 people work in her husband Neal's office. Each office is giving away five prizes. What is the probability that Raynel or Neal will win a prize?

(A) $\frac{1}{6}$

(B) $\frac{2}{25}$

(C) $\frac{2}{75}$

(D) $\frac{10}{125}$

2. In exercise 1, what is the probability of both Raynel and Neal winning prizes? Remember that they are in different offices.

(F) $\frac{5}{75}$

(G) $\frac{5}{50}$

(H) $\frac{1}{150}$

(J) $\frac{2}{125}$

3. A box contains 63 marbles. In the box are 21 brown, 21 purple, and 21 white marbles. What is the probability of picking a brown marble, returning it, and picking a white marble?

(A) $\frac{2}{3}$

(B) $\frac{1}{3}$

(C) $\frac{1}{9}$

(D) $\frac{1}{21}$

4. In exercise 3, what is the probability of picking a purple marble on the first attempt or a brown marble on the second attempt?

(F) $\frac{2}{3}$

(G) $\frac{1}{3}$

(H) $\frac{1}{9}$

(J) $\frac{1}{21}$

Math
3.5

Statistics, Data Analysis,
and Probability

Independent and Dependent Events

Example:

Flipping two coins is an example of _____.

Ⓐ independent events

Ⓑ dependent events

Answer: Ⓐ

DIRECTIONS: Choose the best answer.

1. Pulling a card out of a stack and pulling a second card without replacing the first is an example of _____.

   Ⓐ independent events

   Ⓑ dependent events

2. Picking teams for basketball is an example of _____.

   Ⓕ independent events

   Ⓖ dependent events

3. Pulling socks out of a drawer is an example of _____.

   Ⓐ independent events

   Ⓑ dependent events

4. A spinner has 4 equal sectors colored yellow, blue, green, and red. After spinning the spinner, what is the probability of landing on red and then spinning again and landing on green? This is an example of _____.

   Ⓕ independent events

   Ⓖ dependent events

5. A 6-sided die is rolled. What is the probability of rolling an even number and then an odd number? This is an example of _____.

   Ⓐ independent events

   Ⓑ dependent events

6. A glass jar contains 6 red, 5 green, 8 blue, and 3 yellow marbles. If a single marble is chosen at random from the jar, what is the probability that it is red and a second marble drawn is blue? This is an example of _____.

   Ⓕ independent events

   Ⓖ dependent events

7. Choose a number at random from 1 to 5. What is the probability that the first number chosen is even and the second number chosen is odd? This is an example of _____.

   Ⓐ independent events

   Ⓑ dependent events

8. A dresser drawer contains one pair of socks of each of the following colors: blue, brown, red, white and black. Each pair is folded together in matching sets. You reach into the sock drawer and choose a pair of socks without looking. The first pair you pull out is red -the wrong color. You replace this pair and choose another pair. What is the probability that you will get the red pair of socks twice? This is an example of _____.

   Ⓕ independent events

   Ⓖ dependent events

158

Math
3.0

Mini-Test 3

For pages 154–158

DIRECTIONS: Choose the best answer.

1. The sweaters on sale come in three styles: pullover, cardigan, and turtleneck. The come in three colors: black, white, and red. How many choices are there?
   - (A) 9
   - (B) 6
   - (C) 3
   - (D) 12

2. For question 1, what is the probability of choosing a black pullover?
   - (F) $\frac{1}{12}$
   - (G) $\frac{1}{9}$
   - (H) $\frac{1}{6}$
   - (J) $\frac{1}{3}$

3. Williamson's batting average is 0.181. How many hits did he average in 10 times at bat?
   - (A) 0
   - (B) 1
   - (C) 2
   - (D) 3

4. LaRue has a batting average of 0.249. How many hits should he have in the next 100 times at bat?
   - (F) 249
   - (G) 25
   - (H) 3
   - (J) 10

For questions 5–6, assume that an equal number of people are born in each month.

5. If you try to guess the month someone was born, what is the probability that you will guess the correct month?
   - (A) $\frac{1}{12}$
   - (B) $\frac{1}{6}$
   - (C) $\frac{1}{24}$
   - (D) $\frac{1}{13}$

6. Suppose you are at a party with 35 people. You say that you can guarantee that you will find two people who were born in the same month if you can ask a certain number of people in what month he or she was born. What is the smallest number of people you can ask?
   - (F) 6
   - (G) 12
   - (H) 13
   - (J) 20

7. A coin is tossed and a single 6-sided die is rolled. Find the probability of getting a head on the coin and a 3 on the die. This is an example of _____.
   - (A) independent events
   - (B) dependent events

How Am I Doing?

Mini-Test 1 Page 145 **Number Correct** ☐	**7–8** answers correct	**Great Job!** Move on to the section test on page 161.
	4–6 answers correct	**You're almost there!** But you still need a little practice. Review practice pages 141–144 before moving on to the section test on page 161.
	0–3 answers correct	**Oops!** Time to review what you have learned and try again. Review the practice section on pages 141–144. Then retake the test on page 145. Now move on to the section test on page 161.
Mini-Test 2 Page 152 **Number Correct** ☐	**8–9** answers correct	**Awesome!** Move on to the section test on page 161.
	5–7 answers correct	**You're almost there!** But you still need a little practice. Review practice pages 147–151 before moving on to the section test on page 161.
	0–4 answers correct	**Oops!** Time to review what you have learned and try again. Review the practice section on pages 147–151. Then retake the test on page 152. Now move on to the section test on page 161.
Mini-Test 3 Page 159 **Number Correct** ☐	**6–7** answers correct	**Great Job!** Move on to the section test on page 161.
	3–5 answers correct	**You're almost there!** But you still need a little practice. Review practice pages 154–158 before moving on to the section test on page 161.
	0–2 answers correct	**Oops!** Time to review what you have learned and try again. Review the practice section on pages 154–158. Then retake the test on page 159. Now move on to the section test on page 161.

Name _____   Date _____

Final Statistics, Data Analysis, and Probability Test
for pages 141–159

DIRECTIONS: Choose the best answer.

1. **Find the mode for 85, 105, 135, 85, and 65.**
   - (A) 70
   - (B) 85
   - (C) 86
   - (D) 95

2. **Find the median for 85, 105, 135, 85, and 65.**
   - (F) 70
   - (G) 85
   - (H) 86
   - (J) 95

3. **Find the mean for 85, 105, 135, 85, 65, 80, and 84.**
   - (A) 70
   - (B) 85
   - (C) 86
   - (D) 91.3

4. **Find the median for 85, 105, 135, 85, 65, 80, and 84.**
   - (F) 70
   - (G) 85
   - (H) 86
   - (J) 91.3

5. **Find the mode for 85, 105, 135, 85, 65, 80, and 84.**
   - (A) 70
   - (B) 85
   - (C) 86
   - (D) 91.3

6. **Find the mean for 85, 105, 135, 85, 65, and 45.**
   - (F) 85
   - (G) 86
   - (H) 86.7
   - (J) 90

7. **Find the mean for 85, 105, 135, and 85.**
   - (A) 50
   - (B) 85
   - (C) 95
   - (D) 102.5

8. **Jenny's grades during middle school are shown in the table. The mean is 2.7 (B-), the median is B, and the mode is B and C. Which average best represents the data?**

Grade	A	B	C	D	F
Frequency	7	6	6	2	1

   - (F) mean
   - (G) median
   - (H) mode
   - (J) none of the above

9. **For the data 22, 16, 31, 30, 34, 26, 28, 22, 15, the mode is 22, the mean is 24.9, and the median is 26. Which average best represents the data?**
   - (A) mean
   - (B) median
   - (C) mode
   - (D) none of the above

GO

A survey by the advertisement buyer MediaEdge has found that 29% of respondents would never switch from analogue to digital TV, up from 21% in a similar survey conducted in October 2001. Sixty percent of respondents over 65 said that they would not switch.

10. **If you were trying to promote digital TV, you would use _____.**

    (F)   the overall survey results

    (G)   the over 65 results

    (H)   another small sample of results

    (J)   another survey

11. **If you were arguing whether a nursing home should get digital TV, you would use _____.**

    (A)   the overall survey results

    (B)   the over 65 results

    (C)   another small sample of results

    (D)   another survey

12. **The Baseball Boosters conducted a survey of students to find their soft drink preference. Which location would give them a biased survey?**

    (F)   baseball field

    (G)   at a table in the cafeteria

    (H)   next to a specific soda dispenser

    (J)   in the library

13. **Talia wanted to find out students' favorite entertainment: concerts, movies, or dances. Which situation would give her a random sampling?**

    (A)   She surveyed a small group of people standing in line at a movie theater.

    (B)   She surveyed every tenth student leaving school at the end of the day.

    (C)   She surveyed every tenth student leaving a concert.

    (D)   She surveyed a group of people on the dance floor.

Amount	$20	$15	$12	$10	$8	$7	$5	$2
Frequency	3	4	3	5	7	1	1	1

A movie theater charges $7 for a ticket. The theater manager is considering raising the ticket price and asked 25 people to name the greatest amount they would be willing to pay to see a movie. The results are shown in the table.

14. **In order to justify a large increase in the ticket price, which measure of central tendency might the theater manager use?**

    (F)   mean

    (G)   median

    (H)   mode

    (J)   range

15. **If theater patrons saw this survey, which measure of central tendency might they point out to the manager to keep the price increase low?**

    (A)   mean

    (B)   median

    (C)   mode

    (D)   range

GO

16. The owners of a restaurant are planning a new menu and want to find out the type of sandwich meat most customers like best. Which of the following sampling methods would give them the most random result?

   (F) Ask every fifth customer who arrives at the restaurant during one day.

   (G) Ask all customers seated at the table closest to the cashier between 11:30 A.M. and 2:30 P.M. on one day.

   (H) Ask all customers served during one day by a waiter chosen at random.

   (J) Ask all customers who call for dinner reservations.

17. To identify the most popular current movie among teens which of the following sampling methods would give the most random result?

   (A) Ask seven students seated at the same table in the school cafeteria to name the most recent movie they have seen.

   (B) Ask every third teenager that enters a movie theater at a certain time their favorite movie.

   (C) Ask every fifth teenager that leaves a movie theater at a certain time to name his or her favorite movie.

   (D) Ask every tenth teenager at the mall which current movie is his or her favorite.

18. Which of the following ads is not based on survey results?

   (F) Three our of four dentists recommend GelWhite.

   (G) ToastPops are eaten by 34% more kids.

   (H) Five out of six kids think Fluffles taste better than that other cereal.

   (J) Whirl-it picks up 45% more dirt.

19. The convenience store has a choice of chocolate, vanilla, and strawberry frozen yogurt in either a sugar cone or a waffle cone. How many choices are there?

   (A) 9

   (B) 6

   (C) 3

   (D) 5

20. For the previous exercise what is the probability that you will choose a chocolate frozen yogurt on a waffle cone?

   (F) $\dfrac{1}{3}$

   (G) $\dfrac{1}{5}$

   (H) $\dfrac{1}{6}$

   (J) $\dfrac{1}{9}$

21. Mateo has a batting average of 0.256. In 200 at bats, how many hits would you expect?

   (A) 26

   (B) 25

   (C) 20

   (D) 51

22. Three of the last four years it has snowed on January 1st in Snowville. How many of the next four years should we expect snow on January 1st?

   (F) 4

   (G) 3

   (H) 2

   (J) 1

GO

23. A writing contest received 500 submissions. All 24 students in your class sent in a submission. What is the probability that someone in your class will win?

(A) $\frac{1}{24}$

(B) $\frac{1}{500}$

(C) $\frac{6}{125}$

(D) $\frac{1}{5}$

24. Greg's company has 175 employees. At the holiday party this year, the company is giving away five prizes. What is the probability that Greg will win?

(F) $\frac{1}{35}$

(G) $\frac{1}{5}$

(H) $\frac{1}{175}$

(J) $\frac{1}{170}$

25. A whole number in the range 1 through 16 (including 1 and 16) is picked at random. What is the probability that the number is even?

(A) $\frac{1}{8}$

(B) $\frac{1}{16}$

(C) $\frac{1}{3}$

(D) $\frac{1}{2}$

26. A jar contains 3 red, 5 green, 2 blue and 6 yellow marbles. A marble is chosen at random from the jar. After replacing it, a second marble is chosen. What is the probability of getting a green and a yellow marble? This is an example of _____.

(F) independent events

(G) dependent events

27. You roll a number cube and flip a coin. What is the probability that you get a 5 or a head?

(A) $\frac{2}{3}$

(B) $\frac{1}{6}$

(C) $\frac{1}{2}$

(D) $\frac{1}{3}$

28. You roll a number cube and flip a coin. What is the probability that you get a 4 and a tail?

(F) $\frac{1}{6}$

(G) $\frac{2}{3}$

(H) $\frac{1}{12}$

(J) $\frac{1}{2}$

29. A drawer contains 3 red paperclips, 4 green paperclips, and 5 blue paperclips. One paperclip is taken from the drawer and is not replaced. Another paperclip is taken from the drawer. What is the probability that the first paperclip is red and the second paperclip is blue? This is an example of _____.

(A) independent events

(B) dependent events

Name _____ Date _____

Statistics, Data Analysis, and Probability Test
Answer Sheet

1 (A) (B) (C) (D)
2 (F) (G) (H) (J)
3 (A) (B) (C) (D)
4 (F) (G) (H) (J)
5 (A) (B) (C) (D)
6 (F) (G) (H) (J)
7 (A) (B) (C) (D)
8 (F) (G) (H) (J)
9 (A) (B) (C) (D)
10 (F) (G) (H) (J)

11 (A) (B) (C) (D)
12 (F) (G) (H) (J)
13 (A) (B) (C) (D)
14 (F) (G) (H) (J)
15 (A) (B) (C) (D)
16 (F) (G) (H) (J)
17 (A) (B) (C) (D)
18 (F) (G) (H) (J)
19 (A) (B) (C) (D)
20 (F) (G) (H) (J)

21 (A) (B) (C) (D)
22 (F) (G) (H) (J)
23 (A) (B) (C) (D)
24 (F) (G) (H) (J)
25 (A) (B) (C) (D)
26 (F) (G)
27 (A) (B) (C) (D)
28 (F) (G) (H) (J)
29 (A) (B)

Mathematical Reasoning Standards

1.0 Students make decisions about how to approach problems:

1.1 Analyze problems by identifying relationships, distinguishing relevant from irrelevant information, identifying missing information, sequencing and prioritizing information, and observing patterns. *(See page 167.)*

1.2 Formulate and justify mathematical conjectures based on a general description of the mathematical question or problem posed. *(See page 168.)*

1.3 Determine when and how to break a problem into simpler parts. *(See page 169.)*

Math
1.1

Analyzing Problems

Clue Read the problem carefully and look at all answer choices before you mark the one you think is correct.

DIRECTIONS: Choose the best answer.

1. At her party, Emily wants to serve each of her friends a hot dog and a bun. There are 8 hot dogs in a package but only 6 buns in a bag. What is the least amount of hot dogs Emily must buy so that she has the same amount of hot dogs and buns?

   Ⓐ 48
   Ⓑ 16
   Ⓒ 8
   Ⓓ 24

2. What number is missing from the pattern?

   2, 6, 14, _____, 62, 126

   Ⓕ 18
   Ⓖ 22
   Ⓗ 30
   Ⓙ 28

3. How much would the value of 456,881 be decreased by replacing the 6 with a 5?

   Ⓐ 10,000
   Ⓑ 1,000
   Ⓒ 1
   Ⓓ 100

4. A number has a 7 in the tens place, a 5 in the ones place, and a 3 in the thousands place. Which number is it?

   Ⓕ 753
   Ⓖ 375
   Ⓗ 7,385
   Ⓙ 3,175

5. What number is missing from the pattern?

   $\frac{4}{10}$, 0.5, $\frac{6}{10}$, 0.7, _____, 0.9

   Ⓐ $\frac{8}{10}$
   Ⓑ $\frac{7}{10}$
   Ⓒ 0.8
   Ⓓ 0.08

6. What is the ratio of four days to four weeks?

   Ⓕ $\frac{1}{14}$
   Ⓖ $\frac{1}{7}$
   Ⓗ $\frac{1}{2}$
   Ⓙ $\frac{1}{15}$

7. Last summer, 6 friends ran their own lawn care business. The friends made a total of $498.54. The friends agreed to share the profit equally. How much did each friend make?

   Ⓐ $73.09
   Ⓑ $83.09
   Ⓒ $84.09
   Ⓓ $79.09

Math

1.2

Solving Problems

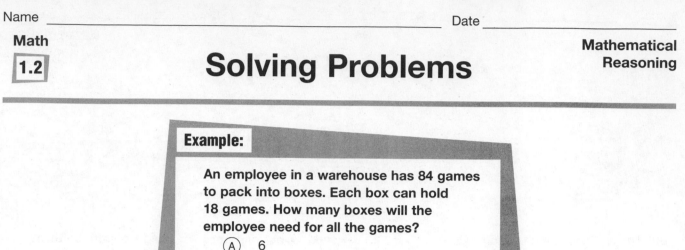

Example:

An employee in a warehouse has 84 games to pack into boxes. Each box can hold 18 games. How many boxes will the employee need for all the games?

(A) 6

(B) 4

(C) 5

(D) 8

Answer: (C)

Clue   Take your best guess when you are unsure of the answer. When you work on scratch paper, be sure to transfer numbers accurately and compute carefully.

DIRECTIONS: Choose the best answer.

1. **Which group contains both odd and even numbers?**

    (A) 76, 94, 54, 32, 22

    (B) 33, 51, 11, 99, 37

    (C) 72, 44, 68, 94, 26

    (D) 55, 38, 21, 88, 33

2. **Which of these statements is true?**

    (F) When a whole number is multiplied by 3, the product will always be an odd number.

    (G) When a whole number is multiplied by 4, the product will always be an even number.

    (H) All numbers that can be divided by 5 are odd numbers.

    (J) The product of an odd and even number is always an odd number.

3. **Pam had 45 packages of licorice and wanted to put them in bags that could hold 10 packages each. How many bags could she fill completely?**

    (A) 5

    (B) 4

    (C) 6

    (D) 2

4. **A soccer game started at 11:15 A.M. and lasted 2 hours and 10 minutes. What time did the game end?**

    (F) 1:25 A.M.

    (G) 2:25 P.M.

    (H) 1:25 P.M.

    (J) 1:35 P.M.

Solving Problems

Example:

What is the greatest common factor of
42 and 54?

    (A)   6

    (B)   7

    (C)   4

    (D)   9   Answer: (A)

DIRECTIONS: Choose the best answer.

1. **Which number is less than 176 and more than 165?**

    (A)   177

    (B)   164

    (C)   167

    (D)   154

2. **A number is less than 443 and greater than 397. The sum of the ones digit and the tens digit in the number is 5. The ones digit is 3. What is the number?**

    (F)   423

    (G)   432

    (H)   323

    (J)   322

3. **Betsy has 7 quarters, 8 nickels, 9 dimes, 67 pennies, and 3 half-dollars. How much money does she have altogether?**

    (A) $8.43

    (B) $5.22

    (C) $7.32

    (D) $6.22

4. **Aleesha saved $0.45 out of her allowance for several weeks so that she could buy a bottle of nail polish for $2.70. How many weeks did she need to save $0.45?**

    (F)   6 weeks

    (G)   4 weeks

    (H)   3 weeks

    (J)   5 weeks

5. **14 teachers and 246 students will travel to the state capitol. One bus holds 38 people. How many buses are needed altogether?**

    (A)   6 buses

    (B)   7 buses

    (C)   5 buses

    (D)   8 buses

6. **13 people ride to school in 2 cars. One car holds three more people than the other. How many people are in each car?**

    (F)   8 in one car and 5 in the other

    (G)   9 in one car and 4 in the other

    (H)   7 in one car and 6 in the other

    (J)   3 in one car and 10 in the other

Name _____ Date _____

Math

1.0

For pages 167–169

Mini-Test 1

DIRECTIONS: Choose the best answer.

1. **Chris put 72 kilograms of jam into jars. He put 0.4 kilogram into each jar. How many jars did he use?**

   Ⓐ 90 jars

   Ⓑ 180 jars

   Ⓒ 80 jars

   Ⓓ 72 jars

2. **Jeremy opened a savings account. He deposited $23.45 into his account. The monthly rate of interest on his account is 5%. How much interest would Jeremy receive on that amount at the end of the month?**

   Ⓕ $1.17

   Ⓖ $117.25

   Ⓗ $17.25

   Ⓙ $0.17

3. **Which of these statements is true?**

   Ⓐ 11 quarters is worth more than 19 dimes

   Ⓑ 50 nickels is worth more than 25 dimes

   Ⓒ 6 quarters is worth more than 16 dimes

   Ⓓ 15 nickels is worth more than 9 dimes

4. **How many more glass balls are needed to fill the box to the top?**

   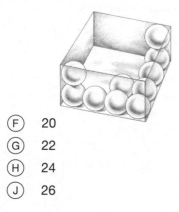

   Ⓕ 20

   Ⓖ 22

   Ⓗ 24

   Ⓙ 26

5. **What is the rule for this number sequence?**
   5, 11, 29, 83, 245, . . .

   Ⓐ multiply by 3, then add 5

   Ⓑ multiply by 2, then add 1

   Ⓒ multiply by 2, then add 7

   Ⓓ multiply by 3, then subtract 4

6. **Which of these is an improper fraction?**

   Ⓕ $\frac{45}{90}$

   Ⓖ $\frac{37}{36}$

   Ⓗ $1\frac{2}{9}$

   Ⓙ $\frac{9}{10}$

7. **Jupiter has 16 moons, Mars has $\frac{1}{8}$ the number of moons that Jupiter has. How many moons does Mars have?**

   Ⓐ 8

   Ⓑ 2

   Ⓒ 4

   Ⓓ 6

8. **Which of these is another name for $\frac{13}{4}$?**

   Ⓐ 4

   Ⓑ $3\frac{1}{3}$

   Ⓒ $8\frac{1}{4}$

   Ⓓ $3\frac{1}{4}$

170

Mathematical Reasoning Standards

2.0 Students use strategies, skills, and concepts in finding solutions:

2.1 Use estimation to verify the reasonableness of calculated results.
(See page 172.)

2.2 Apply strategies and results from simpler problems to more complex problems.
(See page 173.)

2.3 Estimate unknown quantities graphically and solve for them by using logical reasoning and arithmetic and algebraic techniques. *(See page 174.)*

2.4 Use a variety of methods, such as words, numbers, symbols, charts, graphs, tables, diagrams, and models, to explain mathematical reasoning.
(See page 175.)

2.5 Express the solution clearly and logically by using the appropriate mathematical notation and terms and clear language; support solutions with evidence in both verbal and symbolic work. *(See page 176.)*

2.6 Indicate the relative advantages of exact and approximate solutions to problems and give answers to a specified degree of accuracy. *(See page 177.)*

2.7 Make precise calculations and check the validity of the results from the context of the problem. *(See page 178.)*

3.0 Students move beyond a particular problem by generalizing to other situations:

3.1 Evaluate the reasonableness of the solution in the context of the original situation.

3.2 Note the method of deriving the solution and demonstrate a conceptual understanding of the derivation by solving similar problems.

3.3 Develop generalizations of the results obtained and the strategies used and apply them in new problem situations.

Using Estimation

Example:

A number rounded to the nearest hundred is 98,400. The same number rounded to the nearest thousand is 98,000. Which of these could be the number?

- (A) 98,567
- (B) 98,398
- (C) 99,123
- (D) 98,745

Answer: (B)

DIRECTIONS: Choose the best answer.

1. A hot dog weighs —
   - (A) a few pounds
   - (B) a few ounces
   - (C) a few grams
   - (D) a few milligrams

2. In which of the situations below would you probably use an estimate?
   - (F) You owe your sister some money and need to pay her back.
   - (G) You are giving a report and want to tell how many ants live in a colony.
   - (H) You are responsible for counting the votes in a class election.
   - (J) You are the manager of a baseball team and are calculating the batting averages for the players on your team.

3. Sabrina and Sophie together have more money in their piggy banks than Toby has in his. If Toby has $45 and Sabrina has $23, then Sophie must have _____.
   - (A) less than $23.00
   - (B) more than $22.00
   - (C) exactly $22.00
   - (D) between $21.00 and $23.00

4. If $y > 98$ and $y < 123$, which of the following is a possible value of y?
   - (F) 124
   - (G) 108
   - (H) 97
   - (J) 221

5. Which of these does not have the same value as the others?
   - (A) $\dfrac{24}{3}$
   - (B) $\sqrt{64}$
   - (C) 32×0.25
   - (D) 0.08

6. Estimate the sum of 369 plus 547. Round both numbers to the nearest ten and solve. Then round to the nearest hundred and solve. What are the estimated sums?
   - (F) 920 and 900
   - (G) 890 and 900
   - (H) 910 and 900
   - (J) 900 and 1,000

Math
2.2

Solving Problems

DIRECTIONS: Choose the best answer.

1. **Which of the tables follows this rule?**

   Rule: Add 3 to the number in column A, and then multiply by 8 to get the number in column B.

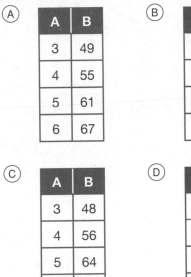

(A)

A	B
3	49
4	55
5	61
6	67

(B)

A	B
3	14
4	15
5	16
6	17

(C)

A	B
3	48
4	56
5	64
6	72

(D)

A	B
3	46
4	54
5	62
6	70

2. **Using the digits 8, 4, 7, and 6, which of the following are the smallest and the largest decimal numbers you can write?**

   (F) 0.8476 and 0.6748
   (G) 0.8746 and 0.4678
   (H) 0.4678 and 0.8764
   (J) 0.6748 and 0.8674

3. **Darnell's speech took $12\frac{3}{4}$ minutes. Tara's speech lasted $\frac{8}{12}$ as long. About how long was Tara's speech?**

   (A) 9 minutes
   (B) $8\frac{1}{2}$ minutes
   (C) 11 minutes
   (D) $9\frac{1}{2}$ minutes

4. **Tony, a novice jogger, in his first week ran $\frac{1}{2}$ mile on his first try, $1\frac{1}{4}$ mile on his second try, and 2 miles on his third try. How far would Tony run in total in two weeks if he ran the same distances the next week?**

   (F) $3\frac{3}{4}$ miles
   (G) $7\frac{1}{2}$ miles
   (H) $6\frac{3}{4}$ miles
   (J) $8\frac{1}{2}$ miles

5. **It takes 5 workers about 50 hours to build a house. How long would it take if there were 10 workers?**

   (A) 25 hours
   (B) $12\frac{1}{2}$ hours
   (C) 100 hours
   (D) Not given

6. **Mike received 65% of the votes cast for class treasurer. What fractional part of the votes did Mike receive?**

   (F) $\frac{13}{20}$
   (G) $\frac{12}{19}$
   (H) $\frac{11}{20}$
   (J) Not given

STOP

Math
2.3

Solving Problems

DIRECTIONS: Choose the best answer.

Mr. Vander's class earned $582 during the school year to purchase new books for the library. The graph below shows the percentage of money earned from each activity. Use it to answer questions 1–3.

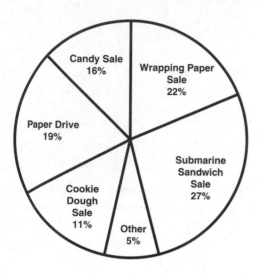

1. **Which fund-raiser earned the most money?**

   (A)   the candy sale

   (B)   the wrapping paper sale

   (C)   the submarine sandwich sale

   (D)   the paper drive

2. **How much less was earned on the paper drive than from the wrapping paper sale?**

   (F) $17.46

   (G) $23.46

   (H) $18.46

   (J) $16.46

3. **How much money was earned from the cookie dough sale?**

   (A) $63.02

   (B) $123.02

   (C) $64.02

   (D) $73.03

DIRECTIONS: The soccer team members needed to buy their own shin guards, socks, shoes, and shorts. Two players volunteered to do some comparative shopping to find the store with the best deals. Use their charts to answer questions 4 and 5.

Sports Corner

Socks	3 pairs for $9.30
Shoes	2 pairs for $48.24
Shin Guards	4 pairs for $32.48
Shorts	5 pairs for $60.30

4. **How much would it cost to buy one pair of shoes and socks at Sports Corner?**

   (F) $27.22

   (G) $57.54

   (H) $31.47

   (J) $28.22

Sam's Soccer Corner

Socks	2 pairs for $6.84
Shoes	3 pairs for $84.15
Shin Guards	5 pairs for $35.70
Shorts	4 pairs for $36.36

5. **How much would it cost to buy one pair of shoes and socks at Sam's Soccer Corner?**

   (A) $27.22

   (B) $31.47

   (C) $29.11

   (D) $31.57

Math
2.4

Mathematical Language
and Reasoning

DIRECTIONS: Choose the best answer.

1. The point where two sides of an angle meet is called _____.

(A) the vertex

(B) the circumference

(C) an acute angle

(D) a ray

2. Which of these would you use to draw a circle?

(F) compass

(G) protractor

(H) ruler

(J) graph

3. The measure of the amount of liquid a glass can hold is called its _____.

(A) volume

(B) capacity

(C) circumference

(D) inside surface area

4. What is not shown in the diagram?

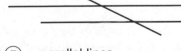

(F) parallel lines

(G) intersecting lines

(H) line segment

(J) perpendicular lines

5. What fraction of a pound is 4 ounces?

(A) $\frac{1}{8}$

(B) $\frac{1}{4}$

(C) $\frac{1}{2}$

(D) $\frac{1}{5}$

6. A map scale shows that 1 inch equals 8 miles. About how long would a section of highway be that is 4.5 inches on the map?

(F) 36 miles

(G) 32.5 miles

(H) 30 miles

(J) 18 miles

7. Which unit of measure would be best to use when weighing an adult elephant?

(A) pounds

(B) grams

(C) kilograms

(D) tons

Name _____ Date _____

Mathematical Language

DIRECTIONS: Choose the best answer.

1. Which of the following lines are parallel?

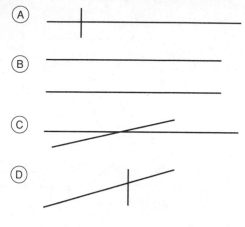

2. A plane figure with 6 sides is called _____.

(F) an apex

(G) an octagon

(H) a hexagon

(J) a pentagon

3. At the school store, Todd bought 6 pens for 59¢ each and 8 pencils for 19¢ each. How much did he spend all together?

(A) $506.00

(B) $50.60

(C) $5.06

(D) $0.506

4. A cube has a side that measures 25 centimeters. What is the total volume of the cube?

(F) 15,625 cubic cm

(G) 625 cubic cm

(H) 300 cubic cm

(J) 50 cubic cm

25 centimeters

5. Which of these graphs best shows how the perimeter of a square is related to length of a side of the square?

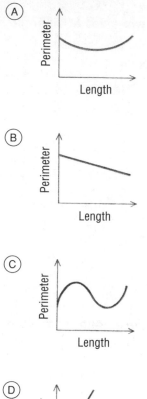

STOP

Math
2.6

Exact and Approximate Reasoning

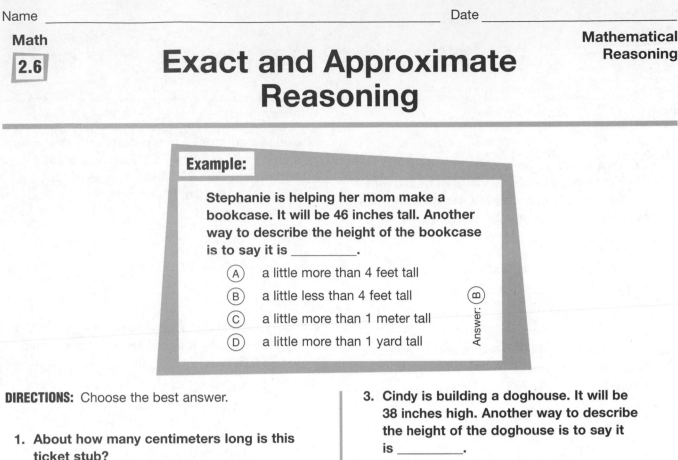

Example:

Stephanie is helping her mom make a bookcase. It will be 46 inches tall. Another way to describe the height of the bookcase is to say it is _____.

Ⓐ a little more than 4 feet tall

Ⓑ a little less than 4 feet tall   Ⓑ

Ⓒ a little more than 1 meter tall

Ⓓ a little more than 1 yard tall

Answer: Ⓑ

DIRECTIONS: Choose the best answer.

1. **About how many centimeters long is this ticket stub?**

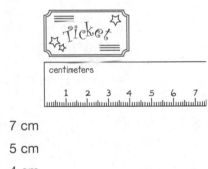

Ⓐ 7 cm

Ⓑ 5 cm

Ⓒ 4 cm

Ⓓ 6 cm

2. **Mary has 6 apples, Sara has 5 oranges, and Kate has 4 bananas. What fraction of the fruit does Sara have?**

Ⓕ $\frac{1}{15}$

Ⓖ $\frac{1}{3}$

Ⓗ $\frac{1}{5}$

Ⓙ $\frac{3}{5}$

3. **Cindy is building a doghouse. It will be 38 inches high. Another way to describe the height of the doghouse is to say it is _____.**

Ⓐ a little more than a yard high

Ⓑ a little less than 2 feet high

Ⓒ a little less than 1 yard high

Ⓓ a little more than 4 feet high

4. **Which of these is 0.494 rounded to the nearest tenth?**

Ⓕ 0.4

Ⓖ 0.5

Ⓗ 0.410

Ⓙ 0.510

5. **Todd, Melanie, and two of their friends went out for dessert and soft drinks. Their bill was $23.40. If the four students shared the cost evenly, how much did each person have to pay?**

Ⓐ $3.90

Ⓑ $4.68

Ⓒ $5.75

Ⓓ None of these

Solving Problems

DIRECTIONS: Choose the best answer.

1. Computer headphones cost $13.95. Ms. Jackson wants to buy 24 pairs of headphones for the school computer lab. How much will it cost altogether to buy the headphones?
   - (A) $335.90
   - (B) $334.80
   - (C) $324.80
   - (D) Not given

2. There are 2,464 monkeys in a nature preserve. They live in groups of 16. How many groups of monkeys are there?
   - (F) 154 groups
   - (G) 164 groups
   - (H) 153 groups
   - (J) Not given

3. Mason, Clare, and Clark each bought candy in the bulk food store. The candy they bought weighed 2 pounds, 4 pounds, and 3 pounds. How many pounds of candy did they buy in all?
   - (A) $12\frac{11}{12}$
   - (B) $11\frac{1}{24}$
   - (C) $10\frac{11}{24}$
   - (D) Not given

4. A shoebox is 6 inches wide, 11 inches long, and 5 inches high. What is the volume of the box?
   - (F) 330 cubic inches
   - (G) 22 cubic inches
   - (H) 230 cubic inches
   - (J) Not given

5. Connie earned $6.00 by baby-sitting. She added that money to some allowance she had saved and bought a new video game for $22.79. She had $2.88 left over. How much allowance had Connie saved?
   - (A) $19.91
   - (B) $13.78
   - (C) $19.67
   - (D) $18.77

6. How much change will you receive from $2.00 if you buy a pencil for $0.19 and a pen for $0.79?
   - (F) $1.21
   - (G) $1.81
   - (H) $1.02
   - (J) Not given

7. Todd traveled 1,378 miles from Florida to Connecticut. Melanie traveled 3,095 miles from California to Connecticut. How many more miles did Melanie have to travel than Todd?
   - (A) 1,717 miles
   - (B) 2,717 miles
   - (C) 1727 miles
   - (D) 1,617 miles

8. How much change will you receive from $5.00 if you buy a shake for $1.29, a hamburger for $0.99, and fries for $0.89?
   - (F) $1.82
   - (G) $1.83
   - (H) $3.71
   - (J) $2.83

STOP

Math

2.0

For pages 172–178

Mathematical
Reasoning

Mini-Test 2

DIRECTIONS: Choose the best answer.

1. **About how long is the paper clip above the ruler?**

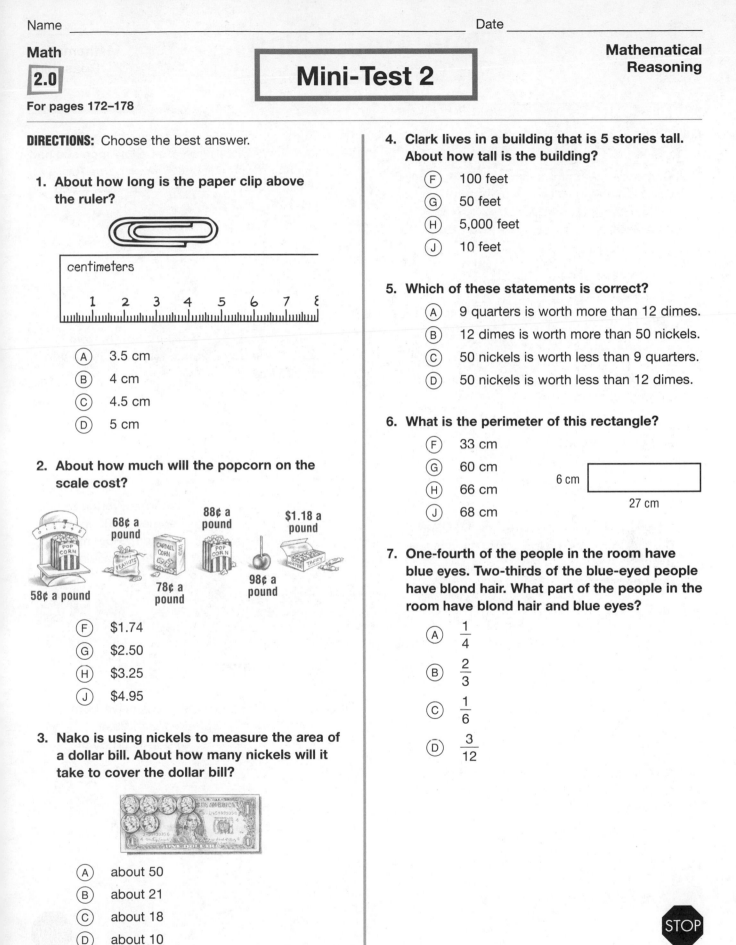

centimeters

1 2 3 4 5 6 7 8

Ⓐ 3.5 cm

Ⓑ 4 cm

Ⓒ 4.5 cm

Ⓓ 5 cm

2. **About how much will the popcorn on the scale cost?**

68¢ a pound

88¢ a pound

$1.18 a pound

POP CORN

CARMEL CORN

POP CORN

PEANUTS

WATER TAFFY

58¢ a pound

78¢ a pound

98¢ a pound

Ⓕ $1.74

Ⓖ $2.50

Ⓗ $3.25

Ⓙ $4.95

3. **Nako is using nickels to measure the area of a dollar bill. About how many nickels will it take to cover the dollar bill?**

Ⓐ about 50

Ⓑ about 21

Ⓒ about 18

Ⓓ about 10

4. **Clark lives in a building that is 5 stories tall. About how tall is the building?**

Ⓕ 100 feet

Ⓖ 50 feet

Ⓗ 5,000 feet

Ⓙ 10 feet

5. **Which of these statements is correct?**

Ⓐ 9 quarters is worth more than 12 dimes.

Ⓑ 12 dimes is worth more than 50 nickels.

Ⓒ 50 nickels is worth less than 9 quarters.

Ⓓ 50 nickels is worth less than 12 dimes.

6. **What is the perimeter of this rectangle?**

Ⓕ 33 cm

Ⓖ 60 cm

Ⓗ 66 cm

Ⓙ 68 cm

6 cm

27 cm

7. **One-fourth of the people in the room have blue eyes. Two-thirds of the blue-eyed people have blond hair. What part of the people in the room have blond hair and blue eyes?**

Ⓐ $\frac{1}{4}$

Ⓑ $\frac{2}{3}$

Ⓒ $\frac{1}{6}$

Ⓓ $\frac{3}{12}$

STOP

How Am I Doing?

Mini-Test 1 Page 170 **Number Correct**	**7–8** answers correct	**Great Job!** Move on to the section test on page 181.
	5–6 answers correct	**You're almost there!** But you still need a little practice. Review practice pages 167–169 before moving on to the section test on page 181.
	0–4 answers correct	**Oops!** Time to review what you have learned and try again. Review the practice section on pages 167–169. Then retake the test on page 170. Now move on to the section test on page 181.
Mini-Test 2 Page 179 **Number Correct**	**7** answers correct	**Awesome!** Move on to the section test on page 181.
	5–6 answers correct	**You're almost there!** But you still need a little practice. Review practice pages 173–178 before moving on to the section test on page 181.
	0–4 answers correct	**Oops!** Time to review what you have learned and try again. Review the practice section on pages 173–178. Then retake the test on page 179. Now move on to the section test on page 181.

Name _____ Date _____

Final Mathematical Reasoning Test
for pages 167–179

DIRECTIONS: Choose the best answer.

1. Which of these numbers goes in the box to make the number sentence true? ■ < 50.05

   Ⓐ 55.55

   Ⓑ 50.50

   Ⓒ 50.005

   Ⓓ 55.05

2. Arnie wants to serve each of his friends a donut and a can of apple juice. There are 8 donuts in a pack, but only 6 cans of juice in a pack. What is the fewest number of donuts and cans of juice must Arnie buy so that he has the same number of each?

   Ⓕ 6

   Ⓖ 8

   Ⓗ 16

   Ⓙ 24

3. Lizette makes cubes from blocks to display kitchen gadgets and cookware in her store as shown below. How many blocks will she use to make Display 6?

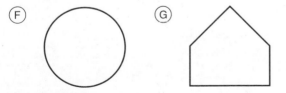

   Display 1   Display 3   Display 3

   Ⓐ 36

   Ⓑ 64

   Ⓒ 125

   Ⓓ 216

4. Which shape is not a polygon?

   Ⓕ   Ⓖ

5. A worker in a warehouse has 68 bicycle tires to put into boxes. Each box can hold 12 tires. How many boxes will the worker need for all the tires?

   Ⓐ 5

   Ⓑ 6

   Ⓒ 12

   Ⓓ 10

6. The number 8 is _____ times larger than the number 0.0008.

   Ⓕ 10

   Ⓖ 100

   Ⓗ 1,000

   Ⓙ 10,000

7. Which of these numbers shows $\frac{29}{7}$ as a mixed fraction?

   Ⓐ $4\frac{1}{7}$

   Ⓑ $\frac{7}{29}$

   Ⓒ $4\frac{2}{4}$

   Ⓓ 0.34

8. A number is less than 539 and greater than 427. The sum of the ones digit and the tens digit in the number is 9. The ones digit is 4. What is the number?

   Ⓕ 463

   Ⓖ 454

   Ⓗ 554

   Ⓙ 418

GO

DIRECTIONS: The graph below shows the average number of rainy days per month in Sun City, Florida. Use the graph to answer questions 9–11.

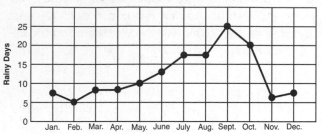

Average Number of Rainy Days in Sun City, Florida

9. **Which two-month period shows the greatest change in the number of rainy days?**

　Ⓐ　May and June

　Ⓑ　June and July

　Ⓒ　October and November

　Ⓓ　August and September

10. **How many inches of rain fell during the rainiest month?**

　Ⓕ　20 inches

　Ⓖ　25 inches

　Ⓗ　about 18 inches

　Ⓙ　Not given

11. **Based on this graph, which two months should have been the best for tourists?**

　Ⓐ　January and February

　Ⓑ　February and November

　Ⓒ　March and April

　Ⓓ　April and December

12. **Sally and Susie together have more money in their piggy banks than Tom has in his. If Tom has $35.00 and Susie has $17.00, then Sally must have _____.**

　Ⓕ　less than $17.00

　Ⓖ　exactly $18.00

　Ⓗ　between $17.00 and $18.00

　Ⓙ　more than $18.00

13. **Two-sevenths of the students in the program arrived Sunday afternoon. Three-sevenths of the students arrived Sunday evening. What fraction of the students arrived on Sunday?**

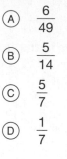

　Ⓐ　$\frac{6}{49}$

　Ⓑ　$\frac{5}{14}$

　Ⓒ　$\frac{5}{7}$

　Ⓓ　$\frac{1}{7}$

DIRECTIONS: The chart below shows how the space in a store was divided among the different departments. Use the chart to answer questions 14–16.

14. **If the total space in the store is 3,000 square feet, how many square feet of space is taken up by packaged foods?**

　Ⓕ　400 square feet

　Ⓖ　550 square feet

　Ⓗ　600 square feet

　Ⓙ　60 square feet

15. **What fraction of the space is the bakery?**

　Ⓐ　$\frac{1}{4}$

　Ⓑ　$\frac{1}{8}$

　Ⓒ　$\frac{1}{5}$

　Ⓓ　$\frac{1}{10}$

GO

16. **What percentage of the space in the store is devoted to frozen foods?**

(F) 30%

(G) 25%

(H) 40%

(J) 12.5%

DIRECTIONS: Choose the best answer.

17. **In which of the situations below would you probably use an estimate?**

(A) You owe a friend some money and you want to pay the friend back.

(B) You are the manager and are calculating the batting averages for the players on your school baseball team.

(C) You are responsible for counting the votes in the school election.

(D) You want to tell some friends how many bees are in a hive.

18. **Which of the tables follows this rule?**

Rule: Add 4 to the number in column A, then multiply by 6 to get the number in column B.

(F)

A	B
2	36
3	42
5	54
7	66

(G)

A	B
2	16
3	22
5	34
7	46

(H)

A	B
2	12
3	16
5	15
7	17

(J)

A	B
2	48
3	72
5	120
7	168

19. **Using the digits 3, 7, 8, and 9, which of the following are the largest and smallest decimal numbers you can write?**

(A) 0.8973 and 0.7398

(B) 0.9873 and 0.3789

(C) 0.9837 and 0.3978

(D) 0.9783 and 0.3879

20. **A basketball game started at 7:15 P.M. and lasted 2 hours and 50 minutes. What time did the game end?**

(F) 9:50 P.M.

(G) 9:55 P.M.

(H) 10:55 P.M.

(J) 10:05 P.M.

21. **A rectangular piece of plywood is 150 centimeters long. It is 75 centimeters wide. Find the area of the piece of plywood.**

(A) 450 square centimeters

(B) 75 square centimeters

(C) 150 square centimeters

(D) 11,250 square centimeters

22. **Each slice of cheese weighs 0.75 ounce. There are 20 slices of cheese in a package. The package costs $2.40. Find the cost per ounce.**

(F) $0.16

(G) $0.15

(H) $0.75

(J) $0.20

23. **A wire that is 0.6 meter long is cut into pieces of the same length. Each piece is 0.06 meter long. How many pieces of wire are there?**

(A) 6

(B) 100

(C) 10

(D) 1

GO

24. A can of fruit weighs $\frac{3}{4}$ pound. How many pounds would 3 cans of fruit weigh?

    (F)   3 pounds

    (G) $\frac{3}{4}$ pounds

    (H) $2\frac{1}{4}$ pounds

    (J) $\frac{1}{4}$ pound

25. The students have $\frac{1}{2}$ hour to complete 3 sections of a quiz. They have the same amount of time to do each section. How much time do they have for each section of the quiz?

    (A) $\frac{1}{6}$ minute

    (B)   10 minutes

    (C)   6 minutes

    (D) $\frac{1}{2}$ minute

26. A hole was dug 12.5 meters long, 10.5 meters wide, and 2 meters deep. How many cubic meters of dirt were removed?

    (F)   25 cubic meters

    (G)   262.5 cubic meters

    (H)   131.25 cubic meters

    (J)   525 cubic meters

27. Suppose in exercise 23 each piece of wire is 0.006 meter long. How many pieces of wire are there?

    (A)   100

    (B)   10

    (C)   1

    (D)   50

28. The distance between two terminals on a television part is supposed to be 2.45 inches. The part is acceptable if the distance is 0.05 inches more or less than what it is supposed to be. What is the range of distances that would be acceptable?

    (F)   2.35–2.45

    (G)   2.45–2.55

    (H)   2.40–2.50

    (J)   2.40–2.45

29. Which of these statements is true about the number 378,654?

    (A)   It has a 3 in the thousands place and a 4 in the ones place.

    (B)   It has a 7 in the ten thousands place and a 6 in the tens place.

    (C)   It has a 3 in the hundred thousands place and a 5 in the tens place.

    (D)   It has an 8 in the ten thousands place and a 6 in the hundreds place.

30. Marty made a base hit on 25% of his official times at bat. What is his batting average? (Note: Batting averages are usually expressed as thousandths.)

    (F)   .450

    (G)   .250

    (H)   .025

    (J)   .275

Name _____ Date _____

Mathematical Reasoning Test
Answer Sheet

1 Ⓐ Ⓑ Ⓒ Ⓓ
2 Ⓕ Ⓖ Ⓗ Ⓙ
3 Ⓐ Ⓑ Ⓒ Ⓓ
4 Ⓕ Ⓖ Ⓗ Ⓙ
5 Ⓐ Ⓑ Ⓒ Ⓓ
6 Ⓕ Ⓖ Ⓗ Ⓙ
7 Ⓐ Ⓑ Ⓒ Ⓓ
8 Ⓕ Ⓖ Ⓗ Ⓙ
9 Ⓐ Ⓑ Ⓒ Ⓓ
10 Ⓕ Ⓖ Ⓗ Ⓙ

11 Ⓐ Ⓑ Ⓒ Ⓓ
12 Ⓕ Ⓖ Ⓗ Ⓙ
13 Ⓐ Ⓑ Ⓒ Ⓓ
14 Ⓕ Ⓖ Ⓗ Ⓙ
15 Ⓐ Ⓑ Ⓒ Ⓓ
16 Ⓕ Ⓖ Ⓗ Ⓙ
17 Ⓐ Ⓑ Ⓒ Ⓓ
18 Ⓕ Ⓖ Ⓗ Ⓙ
19 Ⓐ Ⓑ Ⓒ Ⓓ
20 Ⓕ Ⓖ Ⓗ Ⓙ

21 Ⓐ Ⓑ Ⓒ Ⓓ
22 Ⓕ Ⓖ Ⓗ Ⓙ
23 Ⓐ Ⓑ Ⓒ Ⓓ
24 Ⓕ Ⓖ Ⓗ Ⓙ
25 Ⓐ Ⓑ Ⓒ Ⓓ
26 Ⓕ Ⓖ Ⓗ Ⓙ
27 Ⓐ Ⓑ Ⓒ Ⓓ
28 Ⓕ Ⓖ Ⓗ Ⓙ
29 Ⓐ Ⓑ Ⓒ Ⓓ
30 Ⓕ Ⓖ Ⓗ Ⓙ

Answer Key

Page 8
1. C
2. G
3. B
4. G
5. C
6. G

Page 9
1. B
2. J
3. A
4. H
5. C
6. F
7. A
8. J

Page 10
1. B
2. F
3. C
4. J
5. C
6. H

Page 11
1. A
2. H
3. D
4. H
5. A
6. F
7. B
8. J
9. A
10. G

Page 12 Mini-Test
1. foolish
2. century
3. cloudless
4. ordinary
5. red
6. land
7. permit
8. melody
9. stop
10. light
11. low
12. positive
13. lass
14. untidy

Page 14
1. D
2. G
3. C
4. G
5. C
6. F
7. D
8. G
9. C
10. G
11. A
12. G

Page 17
1. **Antarctica:** extreme cold; little or no vegetation; not much animal life **Sahara:** extreme heat; lack of water and vegetation; limited animal life
2. **Antarctica:** humans live in buildings protected from extreme temperatures; animals live near coasts where they can find food in the ocean **Sahara:** humans move from place to place and live in tents, some irrigate the land; animals have adapted to the heat and lack of water —for example, the camel can store large amounts of water in its body
3. Students should list several reasons why they would choose to visit either Antarctica or the Sahara.

Page 19
1. D
2. H
3. B
4. F
5. T
6. T
7. F
8. T
9. March 22, 1894
10. Montreal
11. Governor General
12. 1969

Page 21
1. 100-meter dash
2. long jump
3. shot put
4. high jump
5. 400-meter run
6. 110-meter hurdles
7. discus throw
8. pole vault
9. javelin throw
10. 1500-meter run
11. discus throw
12. 100-meter dash
13. pole vault
14. high jump
15. 1,500-meter run
16. shot put
17. 110-meter hurdles
18. javelin
19. long jump
20. 400-meter run

Page 22

Students should properly complete the application form with their name (last, first, middle), address (street, apartment, city, zip code), telephone number, birthdate, and signature.

1. free
2. parent or guardian's signature
3. $1.00 per day; 10 cents per day
4. every 2 years

Page 24

1. Northern
2. 70; 5,000; 7,800
3. California, two, the redwood, giant sequoia
4. C
5. Students should write two or three sentences that summarize the author's purpose in writing about sequoia trees. Answers might include: to inform readers about some of the trees' characteristics; or to convey the fact that the number of trees is dwindling.

Page 26

1. if they live on the savanna or in a forest; if they use their right or left tusk more
2. They probably would have become extinct.
3. Someone who captures or kills animals to make a profit.
4. Fewer people were willing to buy ivory. Poachers needed to find another source of income.
5. They again would be in danger of becoming extinct.
6. Students should recognize they need to support organizations and laws that protect elephants to ensure the elephants' ultimate survival.

Page 28

1. B
2. J
3. A
4. H
5. B
6. F

Page 29 Mini-Test

1. D
2. J
3. B

Page 31

1. play
2. poem
3. fable
4. G
5. C
6. F
7. D
8. G

Page 33

1. polite A. She said thank you for inviting her to the party. B. She brought Annabel a thank-you gift.
2. greedy A. She grabbed the chocolates. B. She threw paper on the floor and asked for milk.
3. fearful A. She said she is nervous about sleeping away from home. B. She brought a flashlight and teddy bear.
4. rude A. She calls and invites a boy to the party. B. She rolls her eyes and does not get off the phone.
5. mischievous A. He is hiding at the top of the stairs. B. He is wearing a monster mask to scare them.

Page 35

1. summer; camp
2. see baby possum/by beech tree/second day

    sing songs/in dining hall/every noon

    discover blue racer/in field/fifth day

    sketch plant specimens/in state forest/rainy day

    hear scary stories/in cabin/bedtime

    observe raccoons/in woods/one night
3. Students should use the information from the matching activity and add descriptive details to their summaries.

Page 36

1. A. squirrel, adoring
   B. rabbit, practical
2. A squirrel wants a rabbit to leave her burrow, marry him, and live with him in the trees; she refuses.
3. Answers will vary. One possible answer is "the value of knowing where you belong."
4. hopeful, lovesick
5. annoyed, realistic

Page 37
1. 2
2. 3
3. 1
4. 3
5. 2
6. 2
7. 3
8. 1
9. 3
10. 1

Page 38
1. Lee is compassionate and hard-working. He has been campaigning for several weeks, and his actions reveal that he is concerned with the environment and other people's needs.
2. Kim is not as hard-working as Lee. She is more self-centered and selfish about her goals.
3. Some students might answer that Lee will win because his motives are more sincere.
4. People who are hard-working and unselfish will succeed over those who are not.
5. Hard work and concern for others is not always rewarded.

Page 40
1. Rowan's pony is "little larger than a dog." She is referred to as a "child."
2. He is described as being "evil" and having a "huge form." When he speaks, the story says "he roared." One of the horsemen trembles in his presence.
3. Rowan calls the horsemen "raiders." The person who let her escape was punished. The lord says "Be at ready with your blade."
4. Students should draw a picture of what the oak tree swallowing the five horsemen looks like.

Page 41
1. B
2. G
3. A

Page 42 Mini-Test
1. K
2. E
3. F
4. B
5. D
6. I
7. H
8. J
9. A
10. G
11. M
12. L
13. C

Page 44 Final Reading Test
1. C
2. G
3. D
4. H
5. D
6. G
7. A
8. H
9. D
10. H
11. D
12. F
13. D
14. F
15. B
16. G
17. A
18. J
19. A
20. G
21. D
22. J
23. D
24. J

Page 50
1. A
2. G
3. A
4. G
5. C
6. J
7. C
8. G
9. A

Page 51
Compositions should include a clear statement of purpose. Students should define and defend their opinions with at least two supporting details. Compositions should conclude with a summary statement.

Page 53
I.A. rescues dogs from animal shelter
   C. educating the public
II.A. hearing impaired
   B. individuals with physical disabilities
   C. individuals with multiple disabilities
III.A. Basic obedience training
   1. learn to respond to commands
   2. learn to respond to six sounds
   B. Advanced training
   1. geared to individual person's needs
   2. learn to pick up dropped objects, close doors, and serve as walking support
   C. Training at recipient's home
   1. learns to bond with new owner
   2. learns commands and needs of owner

Page 54
1. D
2. G
3. A

Page 55 Mini-Test
1. B
2. G
3. C
4. F

Page 57

Students should write a short story that has an adequately developed plot and setting. The point of view should be appropriate to the type of story. The story should include sensory details used in a way that develops the plot and characters. Students should use at least one narrative device, such as dialogue, suspense, or figurative language to help enhance their plot. The story should have a clear beginning, middle, and end.

Page 58

Students' compositions should provide at least three examples of the effects of cellular phones on society. Each example should be supported with at least one detail or sample.

Page 60

Students should use the facts about Mozart to compose a one-page research report. Facts should be organized logically and in a way that supports the main idea. Facts that do not support the main idea should not be included.

Bibliography:

Great Composers of Our Time, Brownberry Publishing, 1999.

Christopher, "The Essential Amadeus," Classical Music Magazine, vol. 34, May 2002, p. 29–30.

Zurich, Stephanie, "The Music of Mozart," World Facts Encyclopedia, 1999, vol.10, p. 136–137.

Page 61

1. spelling bee
2. B
3. H
4. B
5. G

Page 62

Students should write a persuasive composition in response to the prompt "The world would be a better place without . . ." Students should state their position clearly and then present at least three reasons why they made their assertions. Their writing should demonstrate that they have considered and addressed points on which others may disagree.

Page 63 Mini-Test

1. D
2. G
3. C
4. H
5. B

Page 65 Final Writing Test

1. A
2. G
3. D
4. G
5. A
6. F
7. C
8. J
9. B
10. F
11. B
12. H
13. B
14. G
15. C
16. H
17. C
18. H
19. A

Page 72

1. C
2. S
3. C
4. S
5. S
6. C
7. B
8. F
9. A

Page 73

1. have or had
2. had
3. will have
4. had or has
5. had
6. have or had
7. has or had
8. has
9. has or had
10. will have or had
11. has or had
12. will have
13. had
14. had or have
15. have
16. seem
17. wants
18. likes
19. need
20. enjoy
21. are
22. works

Page 74

1. car, and
2. ahead; I
3. up, and
4. me; I
5. flying, but
6. Marcy, but
7. stop, or
8. splash; all
9. world, and
10. splash, but
11. Sincerely,
12. Dear Sir:
13. Dear (friend's name, or other greeting),
14. Dear Ms. Sorenson:
15. Dear Julie,
16. Hi, (or any other informal greeting)

Page 75
1. Proclamation, Appalachian Mountains
2. Revolutionary War, Quebec, North, Florida, South
3. Stamp Act
4. Boston Tea Party, Tea Act
5. Gadsden Purchase
6. Mississippi River, Illinois, Missouri
7. Mojave Desert, Sierra Nevada Mountains
8. Peak, Rocky Mountains
9. Ohio, Lake Erie
10. Oregon, Washington, Pacific Ocean
11. Battle, Bull Run, Civil War
12. Lincoln, Battle, Gettysburg

Page 76
1. buy
2. cents
3. due
4. it's
5. there
6. here
7. they're
8. read
9. sent
10. its
11. their
12. threw
13. led
14. where
15. your
16. They're
17. it's
18. you're

Page 77 Mini-Test
1. D
2. J
3. C
4. G
5. B
6. They're
7. its
8. Your
9. have
10. has
11. Gulf, Mexico, Atlantic Ocean
12. Missouri, Mississippi Rivers, St. Louis, Missouri
13. Carolina, South Carolina, Georgia, Atlantic Ocean

Page 79 Final Language Conventions Test
1. B
2. H
3. C
4. H
5. B
6. H
7. A
8. H
9. B
10. H
11. B
12. G
13. A
14. F
15. D
16. H
17. C
18. H
19. C
20. F
21. B
22. F
23. B
24. H
25. C
26. G
27. C
28. H

Page 86
1. B
2. H
3. A
4. F
5. C
6. H
7. A
8. G

Page 87
1. C
2. J
3. B
4. F
5. D
6. G
7. A

Page 88
1. B
2. H
3. A
4. F
5. C
6. H
7. A
8. J
9. C
10. H

Page 89
1. B
2. H
3. D
4. G
5. A
6. H

Page 90 Mini-Test
1. D
2. G
3. C
4. G
5. A
6. G
7. C
8. G
9. B

Page 92
1. C
2. F
3. D
4. G
5. A
6. G

Page 93
1. B
2. F
3. B
4. J
5. B
6. G
7. C

Page 94
1. B
2. F
3. C
4. J
5. C
6. G
7. B
8. H

Page 95
1. A
2. J
3. B
4. J
5. B

Page 96 Mini-Test
1. A
2. H
3. A
4. J
5. A
6. J

Page 98 Final Number Sense Test

1. A
2. H
3. A
4. G
5. D
6. F
7. C
8. F
9. C
10. G
11. C
12. H
13. D
14. H
15. D
16. H
17. D
18. G
19. A
20. G
21. D
22. F
23. C
24. G
25. D
26. F
27. C
28. H
29. D
30. J
31. C
32. F
33. B
34. H

Page 104

1. B
2. G
3. B
4. J
5. B
6. G
7. B
8. G
9. D

Page 105

1. C
2. J
3. A
4. H
5. A
6. H
7. A

Page 106

1. B
2. G
3. C
4. F
5. C
6. J
7. B
8. H

Page 107

1. B
2. H
3. C
4. F
5. C
6. G
7. C
8. F
9. B
10. J

Page 108 Mini-Test

1. B
2. J
3. D
4. F
5. C
6. J
7. A

Page 110

1. A
2. G
3. B
4. G
5. B
6. H
7. A
8. J
9. B
10. H

Page 111

1. C
2. J
3. A
4. H
5. B
6. F
7. B
8. H

Page 112

1. 10 minutes
2. 10 minutes
3. 3 mph
4. yes; 5 minutes

Page 113 Mini-Test

1. B
2. F
3. D
4. F
5. A
6. J
7. C
8. G
9. A
10. A

Page 115

1. A
2. H
3. A
4. J
5. B
6. F
7. D
8. F

Page 116

1. B
2. F
3. A
4. G
5. A
6. J
7. B
8. H

Page 117 Mini-Test

1. B
2. J
3. A
4. H
5. B
6. H
7. B
8. G
9. A
10. G

Page 119 Algebra and Functions Test

1. C
2. G
3. C
4. J
5. D
6. H
7. A
8. G
9. B
10. H
11. D
12. F
13. D
14. J
15. C
16. F
17. C
18. G
19. A
20. F
21. B
22. H
23. D
24. G
25. B
26. J
27. A
28. F
29. C
30. F
31. C
32. G
33. A
34. G
35. D
36. H
37. A
38. J
39. D

Page 125

1. A
2. G
3. A
4. G
5. A
6. G
7. A
8. G
9. A
10. J

Page 126
1. A
2. H
3. B
4. F
5. A
6. F
7. D
8. F
9. C
10. G

Page 127
1. A
2. G
3. C
4. H
5. A
6. F
7. B
8. J
9. C

Page 128 Mini-Test
1. C
2. F
3. C
4. F
5. D
6. F
7. B
8. H
9. D

Page 130
1. B
2. F
3. B
4. H
5. C
6. G
7. C
8. J
9. D
10. F

Page 131
1. B
2. H
3. C
4. J
5. B
6. G
7. C
8. H
9. A

Page 132
1.
square

2.
equilateral triangle

3.
rectangle

4.
scalene triangle

5.
isosceles triangle

Page 133 Mini-Test
1. A
2. H
3. A
4. G
5. C
6. H

7.
square

8.
parallelogram

9.
right isosceles triangle

Page 135 Final Measurement and Geometry Test
1. A
2. H
3. A
4. H
5. B
6. F
7. C
8. J
9. C
10. H
11. B
12. J
13. A
14. H
15. D
16. J
17. B
18. F
19. C
20. F
21. B
22. G
23. D
24. J
25. B
26. F
27. B
28. H
29. A
30. H
31. A
32. G
33. C
34. G
35. D
36. H
37. B

Page 141
1. D
2. H
3. B
4. F
5. A
6. J
7. B

Page 142
1. A
2. G
3. C
4. J
5. B
6. G
7. B
8. H
9. B

Page 143
1. C
2. F
3. A
4. J
5. B
6. J

Page 144
1. C
2. G
3. C
4. F
5. A
6. H

Page 145 Mini-Test
1. B
2. H
3. C
4. J
5. B
6. J
7. B
8. F

Page 147

1. It is likely that about 225 students will order spaghetti.
2. This is a good sample because it is random and it is large enough to represent the entire population.
3. You might use a sample because it can be done more quickly than surveying the entire population.
4. Yes, this sample should be larger than 2% of the population.
5. It is estimated that about 36,400 people voted.
6. No, the poll was not useful because it did not come close to predicting the actual outcome.
7. The poll could have been off because the sample was not random or large enough.

Page 148

1. Yes, it would be biased because the students like basketball.
2. No. It is probably mostly athletic students.
3. Yes, this is a good sample because it includes the entire population of one school.
4. No. Most zoo visitors are concerned for animals and are knowledgeable about the impact of poaching on the environment.
5. Yes. This would be a diverse sampling of people.
6. Yes, if it is done over an entire day. Using only one time period could bias the survey toward certain age groups.
7. No. Waiters don't usually like specialty diets since they are more work for the waiters. At a steak restaurant, a vegetarian meal would be a real challenge.
8. Yes. The visitors would be there for a variety of reasons and would probably represent a diverse population.

Page 149

1. B
2. F
3. C
4. F
5. C
6. H

Page 150

1. This should not be used because all of these people like similar music.
2. This could be used since it represents a variety of adults.
3. This could be used since it is a totally random sampling.
4. Yes, because every 10th box is a random sample.
5. Yes. The person filling out the survey likes the cereal.
6. No. This sample includes only boys.
7. D

Page 151

1. The survey was taken in various places all over the U.S.
2. This means that for every 10 teenagers asked, 7 liked their cola.
3. If most teenagers like our cola, you will, too.
4. Yes, it is possible because a national test is not necessarily random.
5. Just because a toothpaste tastes good does not mean it is good for your teeth. Eighty percent implies a lot of dentists, but it could be four.
6. It doesn't say that the cola drinkers continued drinking Koala Kola, and it doesn't say how many people did not switch.
7. The ad implies that you have to "bounce" every morning. What is "bounce"?
8. The term "best" is subjective. Who determines who the best athletes are?

Page 152 Mini-Test
1. No. This age group is not representative of who buys toothpaste.
2. A random list of numbers could be generated by computer; calling every 50th name; every number ending with 6.
3. Yes, as long as it is done throughout the day so there is a variety of age groups.
4. Yes. All of the students surveyed are allowed to be out late enough to see the entire movie.
5. No. The teenagers surveyed all like the sport they are going to see.
6. The ad sounds like 100 dentists are a lot. Compared to all dentists, it is not.
7. A
8. G
9. B

Page 154
1. A
2. F
3. B
4. H
5. Tree diagram should include the following:
   earrings
   - silver
   - gold
6. Tree diagram should include the following:
   black
   - leather
   - fabric
   red
   - leather
   - fabric
   tan
   - leather
   - fabric

Page 155
1. A
2. G
3. D
4. H
5. C
6. J
7. B
8. H

Page 156
1. B
2. G
3. D
4. G
5. B
6. J
7. D

Page 157
1. A
2. H
3. C
4. G

Page 158
1. B
2. G
3. B
4. F
5. A
6. G
7. A
8. F

Page 159 Mini-Test
1. A
2. G
3. C
4. G
5. A
6. H
7. A

Page 161 Final Statistics, Data Analysis, and Probability Test
1. B
2. G
3. D
4. G
5. B
6. H
7. D
8. F
9. B
10. J
11. B
12. H
13. B
14. F
15. C
16. F
17. D
18. J
19. B
20. H
21. D
22. G
23. C
24. F
25. D
26. F
27. B
28. H
29. B

Page 167
1. D
2. H
3. B
4. J
5. A
6. G
7. B

Page 168
1. D
2. G
3. B
4. H

Page 169
1. C
2. F
3. B
4. F
5. B
6. F

Page 170 Mini-Test
1. B
2. F
3. A
4. G
5. D
6. G
7. B
8. D

Page 172
1. B
2. G
3. B
4. G
5. D
6. F

Page 173
1. C
2. H
3. B
4. G
5. A
6. F

Page 174
1. C
2. F
3. C
4. F
5. B

Page 175
1. A
2. F
3. B
4. J
5. B
6. F
7. D

Page 176
1. B
2. H
3. C
4. F
5. D

Page 177
1. C
2. G
3. A
4. G
5. D

Page 178
1. B
2. F
3. D
4. F
5. C
6. H
7. A
8. G

Page 179
1. A
2. F
3. B
4. G
5. A
6. H
7. C

Page 181 Final Mathematical Reasoning Test
1. C
2. J
3. D
4. F
5. B
6. J
7. A
8. G
9. C
10. G
11. B
12. J
13. C
14. H
15. B
16. G
17. D
18. F
19. B
20. J
21. D
22. F
23. C
24. H
25. B
26. G
27. A
28. H
29. C
30. G

Notes

Notes

Notes

Notes

Notes